Don't Dismiss My Story

D1522188

DON'T DISMISS MY STORY

The Tapestry of Colonized Voices in White Space

First Edition

ALICIA S. MONROE AND RUBEN BRITT, JR.

cognella®
SAN DIEGO

Bassim Hamadeh, CEO and Publisher
Gem Rabanera, Senior Project Editor
Susana Christie, Senior Developmental Editor
Jess Estrella, Senior Graphic Designer
JoHannah McDonald, Licensing Associate
Natalie Piccotti, Director of Marketing
Kassie Graves, Senior Vice President, Editorial
Jamie Giganti, Director of Academic Publishing

cognella® | ACADEMIC PUBLISHING
320 South Cedros Ave., Ste. 400, Solana Beach, CA 92075

In loving memory of an anointed educator, mentor, and social justice champion, **Nathan William Monroe**. We honor you! This book is a true reflection of your heart for justice, compassion for humanity, charitable spirit, and unceasing hope for a brighter future. Through it all. ... Through it all.

Brief Contents

Detailed Contents

Testimonials

Reverend Dr. Martin Luther King Jr. famously asked: "Where do we go from here?" My suggestion is that we go to Dr. Alicia Monroe's book, based on my personal experience in using it during her seminar titled "Black Lives Matter: An Ethnographic Perspective of the Movement." As an eighty-two-year-old White male, I was not your average student. I have been engaged in education my entire life, but this book, and this seminar, proved to be the most important and productive educational experience I have ever had.

It was my great fortune to be raised by loving parents who taught me to respect and accept others, which I did, superficially. But Dr. Monroe's book and its exercises enabled me to make a quantum leap in racial understanding and empathy. Specifically, the exercises designed around the concepts of colonizer–colonized jolted me. I had trouble! My immediate response was, "I am not a Colonizer. No way!" But I was forced to reflect, introspectively, and discuss, collectively, these concepts. Then, it hit me! I was not a Colonizer, in the strict sense of the word, but, as a White male, I had benefited from the residual effects of colonization. As I worked through the book's exercises with my classmates, I had similar moments of enlightenment with respect to the educational, social, economic, and legal benefits that were my privileged inheritance. It was a profound awakening for me. And this book will do the same for you, if you take advantage of Dr. Monroe's gift to you, as a student or an educator.

Finally, please allow me to comment on the benefits I still derive, as a student and an educator, because I continue to draw upon the lessons learned from the book. My wife of fifty-eight years, my three daughters, my four granddaughters, and my great-granddaughter closely tracked my progress in the seminar, and continue to do so. I am acutely aware of this and I accept the responsibilities I have to them. I continue to strive to be a role model who personifies a spirit of generosity and who tries to make the world a better place for all of us. Additionally, as an educator, I recently led three seminars during Black History Month. I drew upon the exercises in Dr. Monroe's book this time around, and I had the most successful sessions I have had in seventeen years.

Dr. Monroe, thank you for your gift; it keeps on giving.

Edward J. Dwyer, PhD, Retired (Veteran, Educator, Author, and Consultant)

This insightful book offers a courageous experience that seemingly creates extraordinary and life-altering realizations for whoever indulges in its content. The authors encourage intense, yet welcoming, conversations about a variety of intersectional issues that oppress and shackle the freedom of marginalized groups in America. The narrative channels undiagnosed feelings into concepts that enrich the minds and hearts of the readers.

The book transcends race and offers educational and perception growth to readers of all ages, races, and backgrounds. I found myself growing more aware of my own identity in the White spaces that I have navigated since the early years of my childhood. Personally, this book has helped me face some undiagnosed feelings and opened my eyes to the true transgressions and injustices rooted within the Black Experience. No matter your class, education level, or family background, the history and human experiences elevated in the book will cross both social and economic lines. It helped me understand that no matter the status I reach, I will still have to navigate the presence of my blackness in a White-dominated world and/or space.

This book opens up space for authentic feelings to be explored and provides a platform for critical dialogue and courageous conversations. It normalizes discomfort and offers unapologetic discourse on radical ruptures that continue to plague the Black, Brown, and Indigenous experience. This book has deepened my understanding of the world and has dignified me, as I have now become more comfortable with the skin that I'm in.

Michael D. Nash II, Rowan University, Political Science, Class of 2023; Black Student Union, Vice President, 2022–2023; NAACP, Rowan University College Chapter, Treasurer, 2022–2023; The Men of Color Alliance, Founder & Undergraduate Coordinator, 2022–2023

Grappling with a dynamic sociopolitical state, these authors challenge American institutions and have the courage to do so with naked honesty. There is significant, meaningful American history that must be explored through a critical lens. Where there is light, there is darkness, and the authors begin a conversation that can lead to a road not often taken—one of nuanced, reflective, and responsible acknowledgment.

Through a thought-provoking narrative, the reader is led through a deep story. The audience is challenged to reflect on many major misconceptions about Western culture as a whole. The authors manage to carefully explore centuries of authentic social change and openly discuss how we can become better. Critical dialogue, as the authors say, is essential for human emancipation.

As a student, an aspiring attorney, and a Christian man, this book made me reflect on the power of my voice. The capacity to communicate, critically, to my peers is a gift that all students should be given. I owe it to all those who will come after me to use my voice to remove all barriers that may stand before them. The path forward, the path to righteousness, is lined with those who stand for all voices to be heard.

Carter Laborde, Rowan University Alumnus, Law Student, Community Member

Acknowledgments

As our steps were ordered to undertake this phenomenal feat, we were blessed with a tribe of loved ones and supporters who made this book possible. To these special people, we are profoundly grateful.

Alicia S. Monroe

I thank and celebrate my family for their unconditional love, conquering faith, and unyielding support. To the light of my life, my husband, Tony Sr.; my sons who are my inspiration, Nathan (late), Tony II, and Allen; and my parents who were my models of excellence, the late Nathaniel and Alice Gill. I honor your existence and profound impact on my life. I am grateful for my prayer warriors, Zack and Mary Clyde Rogers, Iris Felix, Shirley Farrar, Diane Gordon, and Lenita Williams. I am thankful to the Allen and Monroe families for being symbols of acceptance, strength, and resilience. To my mentors, Franklin and Brenda CampbellJones, thank you for believing in me and always encouraging me to "put my hand to the plow" and to look and press forward.

Ruben Britt, Jr.

First and foremost, I would like to thank my father, the late Ruben Britt, Sr., and my mother, the late Ida Louis Britt, for their immeasurable encouragement and support. Also, to wife Penny, son Ruben III, and daughter Savannah for their love and support; to my relatives the Britt, Douglas, Gunter, and Broach families; and Shirley Farrar. Finally, much gratitude to my mentors, Paul Clancy, Alfreda Harris, Wayne Embry, the late Gwendelyn Johnson, and the late William Wimberly for their encouragement, guidance, and support.

With gratitude, we acknowledge the students, educators, and those who identify with the historically marginalized groups whose experiences we amplify in this book. We are honored and humbled to elevate your voices in a way that uplifts the representation of all and ushers in transformative change that is meaningful and will significantly advance the greater good of humanity, if it is embraced with authentic truth and fidelity.

Introduction

> If you find a book you really want to read but it
> hasn't been written yet, then you must write it.
>
> —Toni Morrison

Altogether we, the authors, have over six decades of service in the field of education and we continue to shake our heads at attempted educational reforms and institutional changes that have gone awry because they skirt the deeply rooted issues of race, culture, and class that inhibit academic freedom and success for all students. Mindfully we have created the construct of this text and coined it a counter-dismissal narrative. Our book addresses the elephant in the room that everyone sees, but does not acknowledge and earnestly challenge.

We define a counter-dismissal narrative as a construct that amplifies and interrogates societal wrongs. The narrative uncovers ugly truths that have been distorted and/or masked by supremacist mores. It provides evidence of the historical roots and legacy of destruction of historically marginalized groups whose existence is radically dismissed, attenuated, or erased through the power exerted by a dominant group who comfortably coalesce in the privilege and entitlement inherent in a whitewashed colonized society. The narrative thrusts the reader into cycles of self-reflection in which they are positioned to progressively face and grapple with their own biases, perceptions, and reality, which may or may not accept and include an authentic awareness and truthful understanding of different cultures and worldviews. Purposeful engagement in self-reflection will reveal truths that the reader mirrors in their attitudes, beliefs, and actions.

In a counter-dismissal narrative, gaslighting, political rhetoric, and superficial attempts at decolonization are unacceptable interventions for social "isms"; instead, empathy must prevail. Empathy is not a matter of trying to imagine the plight of others; instead, it is an outcome of one's will to be curious and courageous enough to relinquish personal biases and preconceived notions about historically marginalized groups in order to listen, hear, understand, accept, respect, and empower their stories and experiences. A reckoning with stereotypes, colonialist thoughts, and dismissive attitudes must occur in order to provide legitimate space for a true communion of diverse thoughts, ideas, concepts, and norms.

The counter-dismissal narrative safely engages the reader on a personal journey of self-awareness and leaves them in a vulnerable space where they are willing to seek to understand and shift their personal perceptions. The self-work is prerequisite to the creation of an authentically engaged community that encourages individual realities and positions its community members to be agents of transformative change where they, themselves, commit to and advocate for the unshackling of oppressed voices.

The tragic disillusionment of "liberty and justice for all" as the backdrop to modern dystopia is the catalyst for the counter-dismissal narrative. In honor of the multi-hyphenated identities and cultural intersections that exist in society, the intent of the counter-dismissal narrative is to unite rather than to further divide. The narrative features stories that articulate atrocities resulting from the historical and present day weaponization of fear, greed, and power. Nonetheless, as iron sharpens iron to become sharper and more effective, emphasized is healing justice, which is the hard, unattractive required work for impactful authentic engagement. Accordingly, this text is timely as it lays out the purpose, need, and premise for deep, courageous conversations around the constructs of race, culture, and class in an era where society is forced to face the ramifications of social "isms."

The authors integrate vignettes that are real stories that reflect real voices, real truths, and lived experiences that validate the urgent need for the call out/call in transformative change process integral to the counter-dismissal narrative. To call out is to bring public attention to harmful and destructive words or behaviors from an individual or group. Calling in is an invitation to bring individuals or groups together for the purpose of eradicating obstructionism to move the needle toward harmonious, inclusive coexistence. The text further examines the social impact of White dominance and relational self-proclaimed and self-directed allyship. An organic framework that enacts practices of healthy communicative action engages the reader in the arduous practice of self-reflection and unlearning necessary to operate in solidarity with historically marginalized groups.

The book provides practical, critical insight on the power dynamics of race, class, and cultural dominance in today's society. It is for anyone who is brave enough to challenge their own mental models and the personal fears and anxieties that erupt from socializing with dissociative groups. In the academic space, this book is written for PK–20 educators by PK–20 educators for the purpose of examining the status quo and recreating learning spaces and systems that authentically welcome and engage all students and members of the educational community. It is also an essential guide for PK–20 education administrators and faculty who endeavor to cultivate a sense of belonging for all students and establish welcoming learning spaces. Specifically, educators who may resist and be reluctant to change will feel comfortable pacing themselves through a journey of self-awareness, healing, redemption, and hope. Each chapter posits a premise for emancipation and meaningful coexistence of all voices in society. Self-reflection questions and exercises are intentionally placed at the beginning and end of each chapter. An epigraph that frames the content prefaces the chapter, and a vignette that is extracted from the authors' personal experiences clearly designates relevance and demonstrates how the negative impact of oppressive misconceptions and practices are activated in education spaces. The key takeaways highlight espoused thoughts that are essential for the reader to digest, as they progressively shift their own beliefs, attitudes, and actions.

> ... each of us carries a bit of inner brightness, something entirely unique and individual. A flame that's worth protecting. When we are able to recognize our own light,

we become empowered to use it. When we learn to foster what's unique in the people around us, we become better able to build compassionate communities and make meaningful change.

—Michelle Obama

This counter-dismissal narrative strives to justify the need to disrupt and dismantle the generational curses of identity lynching, oppression, and suppression through centering voice as a powerful aggregate of identity. The text unpacks the history and everyday lived reality of the educational process experienced by historically marginalized groups, which defies the essence of individual agency and potential for emancipatory praxis. It unapologetically addresses the root causes of the polarized education system of today and provides a glimpse into the potential for education in the Gen Z and Gen Alpha eras, where the societal benefits of establishing a culture of equity and hope in schools galvanize the urgent need for transformative change.

The Power Dynamic of Colonialism

When a White infant is born in the United States of America, the child's first breath is the polluted air of White privilege/entitlement. When a Black baby is born in the United States of America, the air fills the baby's lungs with the smog of oppression and disenfranchisement. What can we do to ensure the fresh clean air of freedom and justice fills the lungs of both infants?

—Brenda CampbellJones

Introduction

Chapter 1 provides a historical perspective of the origin of colonialism and its impact on education in the United States. The founding principles of higher education in the United States are based on the colonial colleges of the British education system that catered only to White Christian males. Its core principles are based on exclusion, elitism, and preserving White privilege and culture. A number of the early American settlers were graduates from royal chartered universities, and they continued to employ those same principles in all levels of education. From the beginning, the enrollment of these private institutions of higher learning was exclusive. The primary academic programs consisted of classical language and liberal studies. European colonialism has provided the foundation for White privilege that continues to exist in every corner of American society, particularly in all levels of education.

Traditional thought views schools as the major mechanism for a democratic and egalitarian society. However, within the paradigm of education, historically marginalized students are systematically eviscerated and, at best, held to the periphery of participation (Howard, 2003). Commonly dismissed and disenfranchised from high-quality educational opportunities, these students frequently find their cultural and academic identity under attack. Characteristically, historically marginalized students directly correlate personal identity with academic self-concept (Howard, 2003). Consequently, educational disparities have caused a sense of alienation and resistance for these students.

Opening Reflection Questions

Directions: Before reading the chapter, take a few minutes to reflect on and respond to each of the questions below. These questions will help you become aware of your own perspectives, opinions, and experiences.

1. From your perspective, is America still a colonized society? Do you see evidence of colonialism in spaces, systems, or behaviors? If so, where do you see this?
2. Is American education an avenue for freedom or oppression?
3. What does "freedom and justice for all" look, sound, and feel like?

MARCUS'S STORY*

Mrs. Washington and Mr. Brown were having a conversation with another teacher, Mr. O'Reilly, in the teacher's lunchroom regarding Marcus, a Black student in one of Mr. O'Reilly's physical education classes. Mrs. Washington and Mr. Brown are African American and Mr. O'Reilly is Irish American. Mr. O'Reilly said that he would often send Marcus to the vice principal's office because he would walk out of class if he refused to let him go to the bathroom. Mrs. Washington, who was Marcus's sixth grade homeroom teacher, and Mr. Brown asked Mr. O'Reilly if he had ever asked Marcus why he needed to go to the bathroom so frequently. They further questioned if Mr. O'Reilly was aware Marcus was taking asthma medication, which caused him to use the bathroom more frequently. With a look of surprise on his face, Mr. O'Reilly dejectedly replied, "No."

Marcus's homeroom teacher, Mrs. Washington, mindfully planted seeds of inspiration and hope in each of her students. Developing healthy rapport and relationships with her students anchored Mrs. Washington's exemplary teaching practice. In this case, she noticed that Marcus was excelling in all of his classes except for Mr. O'Reilly's class. Further, Marcus's sub-performance in Mr. O'Reilly's class was solely attributed to him being absent during class time because he was often sent to the vice principal's office. As Mrs. Washington reviewed the performance of the students in her homeroom, she identified a disturbing trend of low academic performance for students who are labeled "frequent flyers" because they are thrown out of class, often due to discipline issues. She didn't have the same experience with these students in her class. In her class, these students flourished. Frustrated and bewildered, she thought to herself how each student would thrive if every teacher truly welcomed all students in their class and took time to get to know them better.

The vignette is based on a real-world experience of one of the authors.

Marcus: The Outlook

The U.S. Census Bureau predicts that the United States will become a diverse majority country by 2026 (Duffin, 2021). As the country shifts to a mosaic where more than 50% of its citizens will identify as non-White, schools must then respond to the changing face of America with new approaches to acceptance and inclusion. Alienated sub-groups, which have historically struggled under the weight of the tradition of marginalization, will usher in a call for action for cultural pluralism, which requires a genuine understanding and appreciation of the values of diverse groups. Schools that fully embrace cultural pluralism seek to decimate the strong-holds of White dominance and privilege in order to promote diversity. Students like Marcus, then, have a fighting chance for educational survival and success. Positive academic and social outcomes for these students pivot from being the exception to becoming a national norm.

Educators, often without realizing it, operate under assumptions about student behavior. Marcus was fortu-nate to have Mrs. Washington and Mr. Brown as advocates who affirmed him. Nevertheless, stories like Marcus's pepper American education. Deficit thinking of American educators toward historically marginalized students is pervasive and remains a caustic default.

Historical Fractures of Colonization

> Until we get equality in education, we won't have an equal society.
>
> —Sonia Sotomayor

The premise of the American treatise is individual freedom, equal rights, and the inherent search for "fairness and virtue in humanity's pursuit of improved ways of building social institutions and ordering human relations" (Cronin, 1987, p. 304). Under a democratic govern-ment that seeks to progress the human enterprise, social justice is radically distorted through a colonized lens of privilege. In other words, injustice is embedded in American democracy. Consequently, American institutions mirror the nation's traditions, norms, values, and practices. Schools, as public institutions, comfortably coalesce under the umbrella of injustice. Social justice ensures that all citizens are physically and psychologically safe to fully and equally participate in the equitable distribution of society's resources. America's historical underpinnings of power dominance and privilege suffocate the intent of a socially responsible democratic government.

Traditional colonialist principles and ideologies frame the narrative of education. White privilege has taken Black, Brown, and Indigenous American[1] students from physical bondage to psychological subjugation for the purpose of power, control, and assimilation. The social effects of white privilege have created a sense of entitlement that is ingrained in the mindset of Euro-Americans from childhood to adulthood. White privilege is an unrepentant attitude that stems from a lack of racial and cultural awareness, and a refusal to acknowledge its dark history of oppression and the inequality of marginalized groups. The distinction of White privilege is often unrecognizable to most Whites, because there is no need for them to strive for acceptance and belonging. Their domination over education, the media, and religion have cultivated a Eurocentric narrative in which Whites consciously and unconsciously espouse a monolithic worldview. When confronted about their white privilege by marginalized groups, many Whites become defensive, belligerent, agitated and some simmer in silence. Consequently, they often perceive the "call out" or utterance as combative, confrontational, and disruptive.

Despite monumental advancements in global communications, Whites continue to employ a philosophical narrative of superiority for the purpose of White dominance. Further, there is a preconceived notion of behavioral norms and disdain for people outside European ethnicities. Oftentimes viewing non-Eurocentric people as abnormal, Whites dismiss the need for multiculturalism in education, religion, and the media. One such example is Harvard College, founded in 1636 and later changed to Harvard University in 1639, the

---

1   Indigenous American is the authors' preferred designation of this sub-group.

first college in the United States. Its mission was based on colonial values, and its sole purpose was to educate elite White males. The first Black student to attend Harvard College was Richard Theodore Greener in 1866. He was admitted to the college as an experiment. His successful completion of an earned degree would then open the door for future Black students. Greener earned his bachelor's degree in 1870. However, the caveat to Greener's admission must be understood and critically examined. If Richard Greener did not receive his degree, there would then be no further admittance of Black students to Harvard College.

Villainization: Social Classifications and the Stratified Society

I swear to the Lord

I still can't see

Why Democracy means

Everybody but me.

—Langston Hughes

From 1730 to 1770, a number of religious factions created colonial colleges in the newly formed American colonies. Many of these colleges served Indigenous American people for the purpose of teaching them Christianity. During this period of expansion in higher education, women were not granted degrees until 1831, when Alice Robinson and Catherine Hall graduated from Mississippi College, a school founded by the Baptist Church. Ivy League schools, whose founding principles were once based on exclusiveness, were some of the last institutions to become coeducational. With the exception of Cornell University, which admitted women in 1865, the remaining seven colleges did not transition to coeducational until the late 1960s and early 1970s.

In the nineteenth century, public colleges offered free education to White middle-class males for the purpose of training them to become high school teachers. These newly created institutions of higher learning were often called "normal schools." The major components of the teacher training programs at these institutions were derived from a colonized perspective in which teaching students of color was absent from the process of creating lesson plans and curricula. As traditions of exclusive education undergirded normal schools, these schools were not challenged or questioned regarding the inequities of this form of teacher training. Despite the name change from normal schools to state colleges and universities, the legacy of preeminent entitlement has thrived on the ideology of separate and unequal for marginalized students and educators for nearly four hundred years.

Oberlin College in Oberlin, Ohio, became the first college to admit women in 1833, and two years later it began admitting Blacks. After Emancipation, former slaves who were stripped of their culture, language, history, and lineage sought to expand their freedom through education. Due to racial segregation and limited access to most institutions of higher education, historically Black colleges were created. The first Black college, the Institute for Colored Youth (later changed to Cheyney University) was founded in 1837 in Cheyney, Pennsylvania. Subsequently, Lincoln University was founded in Pennsylvania in 1854 and Wilberforce University in Wilberforce, Ohio, in 1856. During Reconstruction, thirty-seven historically Black colleges were created from 1865 to 1877. These newly developed public and private institutions of higher learning provided a safe and welcoming learning environment that afforded Black students an opportunity to pursue a course of study for a professional career. Aside from providing a challenging learning experience, historically Black colleges and universities (HBCUs) also fostered mentorship, networking, and a sense of community.

Since the establishment of Cheyney University, HBCUs have produced thousands of successful Black professionals in every academic field of study. Currently, 25% of Blacks with degrees in STEM are graduates of historically black colleges (Graham, 2021). Many successful

Black icons of the past and present have graduated from HBCU institutions. To name a few trailblazers, Booker T. Washington, Thurgood Marshall, Martin Luther King Jr, Ronald McNair, Oprah Winfrey, Kamala Harris, Alice Walker, Spike Lee, Katherine Johnson, and Chadwick Boseman are proud HBCU graduates.

On March 6, 1961, President John F. Kennedy issued Executive Order 10925, which included a provision that government contractors "take affirmative action to ensure that applicants are employed, and employees are treated during employment, without regard to their race, creed, color, or national origin." This radical initiative by the federal government became the basis for what is now known as the practice of "affirmative action," which would later expand into every sector of the workplace, including education (MacLaury, 2010). After Kennedy's assassination, succeeding presidents Lyndon B. Johnson and Richard Nixon both issued executive orders to end race discrimination in hiring (AAAED, 2021).

In 1965, President Lyndon B. Johnson issued Executive Order 11246, prohibiting employment discrimination based on race, color, religion, and national origin by those organizations receiving federal contracts and subcontracts. In 1967, he amended the order to include sex in the list of attributes (AAAED, 2021). The addition of this amendment provided enormous career opportunities for women, particularly in education, where they held positions as school superintendents, college administrators, deans, and presidents. Most of the beneficiaries of this amendment were White females, who continue to excel in a field that was once solely occupied by White males (Kohn, 2013). Executive Order 11246 also requires federal contractor compliance with affirmative action in order to promote the full realization of equal opportunity for women and minorities. In addition, many predominantly White colleges adopted the same concept in the hiring of faculty and staff along with revising their admissions criteria to increase minority student enrollment. Currently, college faculty, staff, and administration are still predominantly White—almost 75% of faculty are White, and people of color represent less than 1 in 5 senior positions (Loo, 2018).

Scholarships and financial aid programs were created to attract marginalized students to institutions of higher education. The Higher Education Act of 1965 included a provision under Title IV that offered financial aid for students from low-income households to attend college (Kagan, 2020). In particular, the financial aid program targeted Black and Brown students. In 1972, the Pell Grant Program was created to provide additional financial aid for students from low- to middle-income households (Stritikus, 2021). Despite these radical changes at predominantly White institutions (PWIs), campus life for students of color remained unwelcoming; particularly at colleges located in nonurban areas. Absent from the equation were academic and socio-emotional support programs designed to cultivate a sense of belonging for marginalized students, who were newcomers to the traditional higher education paradigm and learning space.

Inspired by the civil rights movement, Black students at both HBCUs and PWIs participated in protests demanding degree programs that reflected their history, culture, and lineage. The first protest took place at Cornell University on April 20, 1969, where students staged a two-day takeover of the student center. The collective action sparked protests throughout the country. The student protests ultimately led to the creation of Black studies (later changed to Africana Studies) programs. Currently, there are over two hundred Africana Studies degree programs offered at a number of colleges nationwide (Rooks, 2006).

The Pathology of White Privilege

When examining the current status of public education in the United States, it is clearly apparent that the system continues to implement curricula that lack diversity. American education curriculum standards reflect the core principles of colonialism, in which the dominant faction forces its language and cultural beliefs upon minority groups. This kind of oppressive educational practice is deeply rooted in the fiber of the country. One such historical rupture lies in the dehumanization of Indigenous American people by White settlers and dominant oppressors. In the late 1800s, the U.S. government abducted Indigenous American children from their homes and placed them in boarding schools to force them to relinquish their Indigenous identity in order to assimilate them into American society (Little, 2017). This malicious ploy and brutal treatment by the U.S. government traumatized the tribal nations. Indigenous Americans shun Charles Curtis, the first and only Indigenous American vice president of the United States, for encouraging them to assimilate and send their children to the designated boarding schools, where abuse was prevalent (Gershon, 2021). The social, psychological, and emotional trauma of the dehumanization of Indigenous Americans provoked catastrophic disruptions that did not exist prior to the influence of settler beliefs, attitudes, actions, and behaviors.

Despite being described as an institution that fosters educational excellence and ensures equal access to educational opportunity for all, the U.S. Department of Education has primarily remained politically correct in creating ubiquitous policies that address equity in education. The current remit of the U.S. Department of Education includes the following (U.S. Department of Education, n.d.):

- Prohibiting discrimination and ensuring equal access to education
- Establishing policies on federal financial aid for education and distributing as well as monitoring those funds
- Collecting data on America's schools and disseminating research
- Focusing national attention on key educational issues

It has become increasingly clear that there is a tremendous gulf between life inside of schools and the perceptions of that life by policymakers. The ongoing distortion and omission of multicultural historical facts is the accepted norm in public school curricula. The choice to frame the teaching and learning process through the monochromatic lens of a dominant group impairs educational freedom for all students and educators.

What Is Culture?

> Without culture, and the relative freedom it implies,
> society, even when perfect, is but a jungle. This is why
> any authentic creation is a gift to the future.
>
> —Albert Camus

Culture is the system of shared beliefs, values, customs, behaviors, and artifacts that distinguish one group from another. Culturally responsive teaching centers students' identities, traditions, interests, and life experiences. When a learning environment acknowledges students' social and cultural perspectives, students can better connect their current thinking to new ideas.

One of the disconcerting factors that was often overlooked during school busing and the desegregation of White schools was the animus of the White teachers and schoolmasters toward students of color. Most of them had minimal if any interactions with or empathy for Black people. Despite this major adjustment, school districts and government organizations failed to implement appropriate training for teachers, school administrators, and other school officials to prepare for this radical change. Many educators came to their classrooms with personal biases, hostility, cultural deficiencies, and misconceptions of their new students of color. Today, many of those same mindsets remain prevalent in U.S. school districts and, more importantly, in the classroom.

Addressing these issues is the culturally proficient response. Cultural proficiency is a mindset or a state of being in which an individual or organization esteems the cultures of others, which may be viewed as different, while maintaining appreciation of the values and views of the individual or overall group. As cultural proficiency is the mindset, educational equity is the process that recognizes and considers the disadvantages of students regardless of their social categorizations. Educational equity bolsters support frameworks and models designed to ensure that all students attain the same quality of education. Educators are expected to proactively take the necessary steps to level the playing field for all students by aggressively striving to ensure that every student will emerge with a high-quality educational experience. The shift starts from the "inside-out," when individuals and the organization intentionally engage in transformational processes to affect change (Campbell-Jones et al., 2010, p. 11).

Teacher Preparation

In a 2007 study, the National Comprehensive Center for Teacher Quality found that 76% of new teachers said they were trained to teach ethnically diverse students; however, less than 40% said the training was helpful (Great Schools Staff, 2010). Over a decade later, this data still rings true. If schools do not invest in high-quality professional development that emphasizes culturally responsive teaching, many teachers will be underprepared to create a learning environment that promotes equity and supports all students. It is important to remember that diversity is not solely about race. Culturally responsive teaching prioritizes analysis of academic performance that recognizes the intersections of race, ethnicity, gender, sexual orientation, religion, socioeconomic status, and diversabilities.

For educators, it's imperative to understand the generational culture of students. When there is a void in the cultural channels of communication between the teacher and the student, there is little to no teacher-student connection. Consequently, the learning process is obstructed. Relevant and engaging educators are committed to co-creating healthy relationships with all students. These educators support student voice as central and essential to interactions.

Students intuitively know when a teacher accepts and respects them. Positive teacher-student relationships are especially salient for historically marginalized student populations, which are more apt to experience environmental risk factors that impede their academic achievement and social growth. The manner in which these students reveal and unpack their identities in learning spaces must be understood by educators in order to respond to the needs, interests, and future ambitions of all students. Aside from creating interactive lesson plans that are innovative and culturally relevant, teachers must include engaging career exploration content that is rigorous, progressive, and promising for each student.

Multicultural Curricula

By 2026, America, for the first time in its history, will be a "diverse-majority" country (Duffin, 2021). Further, as PK–16 education welcomes Gen Z-ers, who identify as the most ethnically diverse generation, the traditional Eurocentric system of American education will be compelled to shift the status quo in order to meet the needs of an ever-evolving diverse student population. As the demographics in America shift, it is imperative for the U.S. Department of Education to make radical changes in order to ensure educational progress for all students. Accordingly, multicultural education, in its truest form, should be a requirement and not a choice for school districts. Also, higher education institutions that receive federal funding must be held to the same standards.

For the past twenty years, there has been a sizable shift in the student demographic in K–12 public schools, where 53% of the student population are students of color, in contrast to 79% percent of the teachers in public schools who are White (NCES, 2021). The lack of alignment of student/teacher social categorizations leads to gaps in understanding.

Research reveals that when students learn more about their history and culture, they generally excel in the classroom. In addition, studies indicate that in schools where there is a diverse teaching staff and culturally relevant curricula, students are more engaged in class. The academic performance of all student sub-groups improves overall, and in turn, the number of student discipline incidents declines. More importantly, multicultural curricula reintroduce relevance in education, which plays a significant role in how students see themselves, think, feel, live, and envision their position in society while expanding their worldviews (Sleeter & Zavala, 2020).

Multicultural literacy is a core competency teachers must possess. Beginning with normal schools, prospective teachers were trained based on Eurocentric doctrine and practice. Education is defined as knowledge received through schooling or instruction. However, the parochial effect of a colonized paradigm stifles the creation and authentic implementation of multicultural curricula. In addition to teaching specific content, the purpose of education is to provide students with a broader perspective of social and multicultural views as well as soft skills. Contrary to its intent, education often deprives students of the opportunity to develop an understanding, appreciation, and respect for diversity, inclusion, and multiculturalism because the definition of academic freedom is constructed through a myopic Eurocentric lens. The indoctrination of Eurocentric ideologies in education has a profound impact on the educational experience of Black, Brown, and Indigenous American students. Marginalized students are reluctant to learn when they have little to no positive influences or role models who look like them and represent their culture.

Multicultural education provides a vision of success along with a medium of hope for the voiceless. Today's educators need to be cutting edge when creating and implementing their lesson plans. Teachers must also challenge their students and teach them life skills to help them succeed in an ever-changing world. In a nation that is deemed a global superpower, innovation for reimagining and recreating an educational system that is beneficial for all students is highly attainable.

Deep Dive the DNA

The current status of education in the United States reflects its embryonic origin. Solely developed from Eurocentric ideologies, America's education system continues to value and espouse colonialist schools of thought. Disturbingly, White privilege, which smothers education emancipation for diverse and multicultural philosophies, beliefs, and thoughts, prevails. Specifically, in higher education, the power dynamics of elitism, nepotism, and many other dimensions of oppression contaminate fair and just decision-making; White men dominate senior leadership roles. Among college presidents in the United States, 68.5% are White and 52.4% are men (Zippia, 2022). The race and gender disparities in higher education leadership and management roles become even more apparent as one deeply examines an institution's organizational hierarchy.

The constructs of privilege and entitlement are devastatingly polarizing. Conditions of dominance and superiority are oppressive. Reflective of the civil rights movement of the 1960s when Jim Crow laws were eradicated, White privilege can only be dissipated when there are functioning transformative systems of change that mindfully make space for critical reflection, discomfort, and social consciousness.

What Did We Learn in This Chapter?
A List of Key Takeaways

- ✓ The founding principles of American education were solely based on exclusivity that discriminated against women and people of color. The historical examination investigates the colonization of American education and its continued existence.
- ✓ Race, culture, and class dominance is a subversive norm inculcated in American society. The oppressive power and authority of settlers identified as colonizers frames American education. This chapter examines White privilege and the subjugation of non-White students.
- ✓ Self-awareness is an important component for promoting diversity and equity in the classroom. Raising the awareness of multiculturalism is imperative and cultural competence will help to eradicate cultural ignorance.
- ✓ The intersections of race, gender, socioeconomic status, and other influences continue to have a profound effect on American education.

Closing Reflection Questions

Directions: Consider what you have learned in this chapter as you respond to the questions below. Be aware of how new information and understandings can help you reframe your ideas and opinions.

- ✓ How do you think personal perceptions and beliefs impact expectations, attitudes, and treatment of people from diverse groups of society?
- ✓ Do you think it's possible for people to be in the same place but experience different realities? Give an example to support your answer.
- ✓ Describe your vision of an inclusive high-quality learning experience. What does this experience look, sound, and feel like in a classroom?

References

AAAED (American Association for Access, Equity and Diversity). (2021). *Affirmative action policies throughout history.* https://www.aaaed.org/aaaed/History_of_Affirmative_Action.asp

CampbellJones, F., CampbellJones, B., & Lindsey, R. (2010). *The cultural proficiency journey: Moving beyond ethical barriers to profound school change.* Corwin Press.

Cronin, T. (1987). Leadership and democracy. In J. T. Wren (Ed.), *The leader's companion* (pp. 303–309). The Free Press.

Duffin, E. (2021). *U.S. population by generation, 2020.* Statista Research Department. https://www.statista.com/statistics/797321/us-population-by-generation/

Gershon, L. (2021, January 13). Who was Charles Curtis, the first vice president of color? *Smithsonian Magazine.* https://www.smithsonianmag.com/history/who-was-charles-curtis-first-non-white-vice-president-180976742/

Graham, M. (2021). HBCUs are producing Black STEM professionals—But PWIs aren't matching that energy. *AfroTech.* https://afrotech.com/hbcus-black-stem-professionals

Great Schools Staff. (2010). How important is cultural diversity at your school? *GreatSchools.org*. https://www.greatschools.org/gk/articles/cultural-diversity-at-school/

Howard, T. (2003). "A tug of war for our minds": African American high school students' perceptions of their academic identities and college aspirations. *The High School Journal, 87*(1), 5.

Kagan, J. (2020). Title IV of Higher Education Act of 1965. *Investopedia.com*. https://www.investopedia.com/terms/h/higher-education-act-of-1965-hea.asp

Kohn, S. (2013). Affirmative action has helped White women more than anyone. *Time Magazine*. https://time.com/4884132/affirmative-action-civil-rights-white-women/?amp=true

Little, B. (2017). How boarding schools tried to kill the Indian through assimilation. *History.com*. https://www.history.com/news/how-boarding-schools-tried-to-kill-the-indian-through-assimilation

Loo, B. (2018). Education in America. *World Education News and Review*. https://wenr.wes.org/2018/06/education-in-the-united-states-of-america

MacLaury, J. (2010). *President Kennedy's E.O. 10925: Seedbed of affirmative action*. Society for History in the Federal Government. http://www.shfg.org/resources/Documents/FH%202%20(2010)%20MacLaury.pdf

NCES (National Center for Education Statistics). (2021). *Racial/ethnic enrollment in public schools*. Institute of Education Sciences, U.S. Department of Education. https://nces.ed.gov/programs/coe/indicator/cge

Rooks, N. (2006, February 10). The beginnings of Black studies. *The Chronicle of Higher Education*. https://www.chronicle.com/article/the-beginnings-of-black-studies/

Sleeter, C., & Zavala, M. (2020). What the research says about ethnic studies. In C. Sleeter, M. Zavala, & J. A. Banks (Eds.), *Transformative ethnic studies in schools: Curriculum, pedagogy, and research* (pp. 44–68). Teachers College Press.

Stritikus, T. (2021, November 4). Access to higher education is the gateway, degree completion is the hoal. Doubling the Pell Grant will help. *The Durango Herald*. https://www.durangoherald.com/articles/

access-to-higher-education-is-the-gateway-degree-completion-is-the-goal-doubling-the-pell-grant-wi/

U.S. Department of Education. (n.d.). About ED. Overview and mission statement. https://www2.ed.gov/about/landing,jhtml

Zippia. (2022). *College presidents demographics and statistics in the US.* https://www.zippia.com/college-president-jobs/demographics/

Additional Reading

CampbellJones, B. (2002). "Against the stream: White men who act in ways to eradicate racism and White privilege/entitlement in the United States of America." Unpublished doctoral dissertation, Claremont Graduate University, Los Angeles.

Editors of Britannica. (2014). Hellen Magill White. *Encyclopedia Britannica.* https://www.britannica.com/biography/Helen-Magill-White

Fitzpatrick, C. (2018). *Women's History Month: Pioneers in higher education.* GoCollegeNow.org. https://www.gocollegenow.org/article/womens-history-month-pioneers-in-higher-education/

Flynn, K. (2021). Academic leadership by race. *Investopedia.com.* https://www.investopedia.com/student-diversity-grows-while-leadership-remains-white-5112518

Jones, J. (2019). Richard Theodore Greener—Harvard University. *Black Then.* https://blackthen.com/richard-theodore-greener-first-black-graduate-harvard-university/

Passel, J., & Cohn, D. (2008). *U.S. population projections: 2005–2050.* Pew Research Center. https://www.pewresearch.org/hispanic/2008/02/11/us-population-projections-2005-2050/

Raypole, C. (2021). "Native American" or "American Indian"? How to talk about Indigenous people of America. *Healthline.* https://www.healthline.com/health/native-american-vs-american-indian

Thelin, J., Edwards, J., & Moyen, E. (2021). *Higher education in the United States—Historical development.* Education Encyclopedia, StateUniversity.com. https://education.stateuniversity.com/pages/2044/Higher-Education-in-United-States.html

CHAPTER 2

The Psychological and Social Effects of Exclusive Education

> The American people have this lesson to learn:
> That where ignorance prevails, and where any one
> class is made to feel that society is an organized
> conspiracy to oppress, rob and degrade them—
> neither persons nor property will be safe.
>
> —Frederick Douglass

Introduction

The education system of today reflects its origin, which continues to promote exclusion for the purpose of power and control. Unseemly factors related to inequity hinder the personal and professional growth of people from diverse cultures. This chapter will provide a candid analysis of White dominance and exclusivity, and its psychological and social effects on marginalized people.

Opening Reflection Questions

Directions: Before reading the chapter, take a few minutes to reflect on and respond to each of the questions below. These questions will help you become aware of your own perspectives, opinions, and experiences.

Education, religion, and the media are three systems used to control the mindset of the masses without using weapons or brute force.[1]

1. Journal your thoughts on the quote.
2. How do you define race? What life experiences have influenced your definition of race?
3. What is the connection between racial identity and social and economic stratification?
4. How do you define the "haves" and "have nots"?
5. Do you think American society facilitates the stratification of "haves" and "have nots"?

TYREE'S STORY*

James Smith and his wife, Ruth, are veteran educators. Both have encountered Tyree. Tyree is a highly energetic child, who is always respectful to the adults and the other children at the community center. He often draws pictures in his notepad and converses with the other children. On this particular day, Tyree seemed docile and less communicative with everyone he encountered at the center. Upon observing Tyree's behavior throughout the day, James and Ruth asked Tyree's mother, Sharon, about the drastic change they witnessed in Tyree's behavior. Sharon stated that Tyree was taking medication because his teacher told her he had attention-deficit/hyperactivity disorder. A doctor subsequently prescribed Tyree medication, without any further testing or evaluation. Clearly rattled, both James and Ruth

---

1 Quote appears later in this chapter, in the section "The Impact of Historical Hurts."

shared the staggering statistics of a disproportionate over-classification of Black male students in special education. Further, they emphasized that teachers are not equipped to provide a medical diagnosis. Understanding the racial and biological sorting of students that is a toxic norm of American education, James and Ruth advised Sharon to closely monitor Tyree's behavior and get a second opinion from a medical specialist. They also recommended that she get Tyree involved in activities where he could positively channel his energy (i.e., through art, music, dance, and sports). Sharon followed their advice.

A few weeks later, James and Ruth visited the center again. They noticed that Tyree had bounced back from his sullen demeanor. A smile grew across Sharon's face when she saw them. She happily reported that she followed their advice. Tyree, after being seen by a neurologist, was no longer taking medication. She had also gotten him involved in a few extracurricular activities. Tyree was doing well in school and with his new activities. Sharon also met with Tyree's teacher and the school principal to share what she had learned from James, Ruth, and the neurologist. She articulated her disappointment and dissatisfaction with the teacher's approach to Tyree. Several years later, Tyree graduated from high school at the top of his class and received a four-year academic scholarship from a college in New England.

The vignette is based on a real-world experience of one of the authors.

Tyree: The Outlook

In his book, *Psycho-Academic Holocaust: The Special Education & ADHD Wars against Black Boys*, Dr. Umar Johnson states that one way schools deal with perceived "bad behavior" is to diagnose and medicate students for attention-deficit/hyperactivity disorder, or ADHD. Dr. Johnson further states that when the term attention deficit disorder (ADD) was changed to attention-deficit/hyperactivity disorder (ADHD) in 1987, it expanded the number of children deemed eligible for this diagnosis. According to a Kaiser Permanente Southern California's Department of Research & Evaluation study published in *JAMA Pediatrics*, there has been a 70% increase in ADHD identification for Black children since 2001 (Getahun et al., 2013). Disturbingly, the study revealed that Black boys were diagnosed with the disorder at a higher rate than any other group of students in the United States.

Tyree's classification as having ADHD by a teacher who was not a licensed medical practitioner is startling. And the capacity of the teacher to influence a decision to have a student medicated for a diagnosis that was not appropriately verified is alarming. Students are sensitive to teacher perceptions of their abilities, and they interpret their teachers' attitudes quite accurately (Gandara, 2002). Accordingly, students' assessment of their own abilities can be affected by their teachers' behaviors and attitudes.

The vignette explicitly reinforces the power dynamics that have come to be the natural default for American society and provides an example of how American schools suffer under the weight of society's deeply rooted social hierarchy. In the system of education, historically marginalized students tend to underachieve in the academic realm relative to their nonminority counterparts. It is an unfortunate reality that teachers are more likely to assess middle- and upper-class, nonminority students as having higher ability than low-income and minority students (Gandara, 2002). According to Howard (2003), "The cultural incongruence that exists between culturally diverse students and their school environment frequently results in discriminatory practices such as low-end tracking, low teacher expectations, and an increase in punitive actions" (p. 6.). Further, marginalized students attend unequal schools and lack the family and community resources, relative to middle- and upper-class norms, required for them to succeed. Accordingly, poor academic preparation and the burdens of their social realities typically characterize a dismal life trajectory for these students.

The Impact of Historical Hurts

A people without knowledge of their past history, origin and culture is like a tree without roots.

—Marcus Garvey

The American educational system's ongoing practice of implementing curricula that systematically lack diversity continues to have psychological effects on students of color. It catalyzes students' low self-esteem and self-worth and, more importantly, a prevailing sense of hopelessness. When hope is absent from a student's spirit and mindset, true learning cannot be achieved. Historically marginalized students then author their story from a life experience of anguish and trauma rather than hope and promise. The generational cycle of distrust, trauma, and despair must be broken.

Education, religion, and the media are three systems used to control the mindset of the masses without using weapons or brute force. Of the three, education has the most impact because of its profound effect on the cognitive, psychological, social, and emotional capabilities of children, adolescents, and young adults. According to educational reformer John Dewey the establishment of "the pooled intelligence" of the democratic mind should yield the anticipated outcome of well-educated men and women throughout the world (Piedra, 2018). While most students in public education spend over 49% of the year in school, the ongoing exclusion of multicultural education and teacher misconceptions are correlated with the lack of academic engagement and success of marginalized students (Pearman, 2020).

Understanding that education has a profound effect on the psychological development of children and adolescents, exclusionary curricula and programs of study have stymied the cognitive progression of Black, Brown, and Indigenous American students. Consequently, Eurocentric education has had an enormous effect on how marginalized students think, problem-solve, and see the world around them (Silverman, 2022). In his book *Breaking the Chains of*

Psychological Slavery (1996), Na'im Akbar describes human beings as operating on self-consciousness, while other forms of animal life operate on instincts. Akbar goes on to say that Black students are often victims of psychological slavery in which their limitations rest solely in ignorance. The current educational system in the United States continues to foster cultural illiteracy through the lack of diversity in the curriculum and its failure to train current and prospective teachers on the importance of cultural competence in a learning environment.

The legacy of psychological slavery is evident today. In a February 2020 exposé on CBS News (2020), it was reported that slavery is not included in the social studies curriculum in Alaska, Delaware, Iowa, Maine, Montana, Vermont, and Wyoming, and that the civil rights movement is also omitted in those same states as well as in Oregon. Further, when Black history is taught in public schools, the curriculum primarily focuses on slavery, the civil rights movement, and Black inventors. However, Black history is world history. The omission of a comprehensive worldview in current curricula reflects the intent to disenfranchise specific sub-groups and sustain deficit thinking. As a result, Black, Brown, and Indigenous American students struggle with their identity and self-esteem. The prevailing sense of hopelessness continues to shroud the academic and social potential of these student sub-groups.

Hopelessness: A Failure Paradigm

Failure to meet the needs of all students will continue the established trend of a wide gap in achievement between demographic groups. This trend threatens to maintain, if not accelerate, a class stratification system founded on colonialist principles of a slave state. We see evidence of this trend in the data showing a school-to-prison pipeline that targets student populations for removal from a school environment to a lifetime of incarceration. Nationally, 70% of all in-school arrests are of Black and Brown students (Lynch, 2018). A correlation between school-age statistics and the demographics of the incarcerated population reveals that 61% of the incarcerated population is Black or Brown, despite the fact that these sub-groups represent only 30% of the U.S. population (Lynch, 2018). Further, nearly 68% of the men in federal prison have not earned a high school diploma (Lynch, 2018). This is an unconscionable reality for African American and Hispanic populations, and more specifically school-age males. We currently see disturbing trends of pre–civil rights ideals and practices in the form of voter suppression, stand your ground laws, and questionable jury verdicts freeing killers of young Black males. A tilt in the social system in which the distribution of wealth in America creates a socioeconomic caste system of haves and have-nots intensifies the ruptures of the race, class, and culture.

Discipline Disproportionality

Decades of evidence point to major racial disparities in student discipline rates. Black students in the United States are subject to disciplinary action at rates much higher than their White counterparts (Riddle & Sinclair, 2019). In general, disciplinary actions put students at higher risk for negative life outcomes, including involvement in the criminal justice system (Riddle & Sinclair, 2019). For Black students in particular, the statistics are alarming. The 2013–2014 Civil Rights Data Collection reported that Black students, who make up 16% of enrollment, accounted for 40% of suspensions nationally (Gordon, 2018). Thus, since Black students are disciplined more often and more severely, the tendency for academic failure and hopelessness for these students are indicative of the insidious roots of systemic racism.

Black students are more likely to be seen as problematic and more likely to be punished than White students are for the same offense (Riddle & Sinclair, 2019). A controlled experiment yielded teacher responses to hypothetical vignettes that challenged their perceptions of students. In comparison with White students, teachers were more likely to view the same behavior from Black students as being indicative of a long-term problem and deserving of suspension (Okonofua & Eberhardt, 2015). Further, the U.S. Department of Education's Office of Civil Rights surveyed over 72,000 schools around the United States, which serve approximately 85% of the nation's public school students. These surveys showed that minority students are disciplined more often and more severely, have less access to complex, higher-level courses, and are assigned teachers who are less experienced and lower paid (Carone, 2019). Additional analysis of the data showed that 1 out of every 6 Black students enrolled in K–12 public schools has been suspended at least once, while only 1 out of every 20 White students has faced suspension. The study concludes that the possibility of the school-to-prison pipeline trajectory for Black and Brown students is a harsh reality. There are three trends in public schools that are primarily responsible for the labeling and tracking of marginalized students: zero-tolerance policies, additional and often mandatory referral of students to the juvenile justice system, and the expanding prevalence of school resource officers (SROs) in schools (Carone, 2019). Harsh and biased discipline measures not only criminalize Black students, but these discriminatory discipline practices are also counterintuitive, as they do not resolve the issues they were meant to address in order to produce a safe learning environment, deter future behavior infractions, and cultivate effective parent engagement (Carone, 2019).

The American education system is structured to mill students by groups and label them according to social stratifications. In this case, the alarming result of othering is students who are plagued with self-hatred and low self-confidence, which ultimately has a devastating impact on their academic and social self-concept. Social justice requires democratic, participatory, inclusive, and affirming efforts (Bell, 1997). America's insidious tradition of othering amplifies the hypocrisy of its claim to be a socially responsible democracy.

Imposter Syndrome

Imposter syndrome is described as a psychological phenomenon in which individuals have intense feelings of self-doubt despite their education, experience, and accomplishments. These internal feelings manifest as self-perceived fraudulence and a desire for validation from those in power. According to a study conducted by psychologists Clance and Imes, who coined the term in 1978,

70% of Americans are affected by imposter syndrome. Imposter syndrome is most prevalent among ambitious Black professionals who seek positions and promotions for which they are qualified in White dominated workplaces (Diversity Inc. Staff, 2019). Black professionals are compelled to work two or three times as hard as their White counterparts to prove themselves worthy of a position or promotion. The inculcated principles of the "slave state" continue to frame the perception of success for Black and Brown professionals. Consequently, Black and Brown students shoulder the weight of generations of despair and cycles of poverty. They must overcome systemic barriers that are inextricably linked to race, culture, and class in order to achieve success. Psychologists have acknowledged that the "perfectionism" associated with imposter syndrome contributes to mental health issues, which further complicate the road to success for historically marginalized students.

Black and Brown students experience imposter syndrome, particularly in the classroom. Their need to be "perfect" in the eyes of their teachers and White counterparts affects how they view themselves and often distorts their identity (Takyi-Micah, 2021). In order to fit in with their White peers, Black students have resorted to code-switching in different social settings. Code-switching is a behavioral adjustment used by Black and Brown people to successfully navigate interracial interactions (McCluney et al., 2019). The masking of one's true self is a survival strategy for Black and Brown sub-groups. Code-switching involves adjusting one's style of speech, behavior, and appearance in order to fit in and be accepted by the dominant group. While it is seen as crucial to the success of Black and Brown people, code-switching comes at a great psychological cost.

The Premise of Power

Stories of blatant injustices and indignities pervade our communities. Because injustice has endured for so long in United States, our institutions have come to mirror the theories, norms, and practices of our society (Dantley, 2002; McLaren & Dantley, 1990).

Public institutions such as schools comfortably coalesce under the umbrella of injustice as they reflect the societal norms inherent in the framework of our country.

Dialogue creates a critical attitude. Building effective communication is a matter of blending groups and encouraging a common language. Critical dialogue results from a horizontal relationship between individuals. The two simple line diagrams below represent two very different communication dynamics. The horizontal line, Figure 2.1, shows a reciprocal relationship between A and B, with two individuals participating equally in communication and intercommunication.

Dialogue

A ↔ B = communication/intercommunication

FIGURE 2.1 Reciprocal Communicative Behavior Diagram

In contrast, the vertical line in Figure 2.2 represents a typical system of massification in which A has power *over* B.

A

↓

B

FIGURE 2.2 Anti-Dialogue Diagram

Reciprocal communicative behavior (Figure 2.1) allows individuals to develop mutual understanding and build community together. As a result, critical consciousness will develop between A and B, with both individuals giving and receiving information (Freire, 1987). The horizontal line represents empowerment for all. Critical consciousness evolves from an empathic relationship between A and B in which both individuals actively engage in courageous, collaborative conversations.

Massification (Figure 2.2) requires humans to behave mechanically, with no critical attitude toward their reality. More specifically, the vertical line depicts a power dynamic. By enslaving the thoughts of a massified society, the elite maintain power and control over the ignorant group. The diminished human agency of individuals in a massified society discourages creativity and freedom of choice. Freire (1987) emphasizes that failure emerges from reform measures that are Band-Aid approaches to philosophical and ideological dilemmas. Transformative change that bravely confronts, addresses, and resolves the toxic root causes of massification can eradicate the dehumanization of marginalized groups and a sense of hopelessness that blemishes America.

Gatekeepers

Gatekeepers function as the term itself suggests, as keepers of the gate. However, a more abstract definition of a gatekeeper points to an individual or group that controls access. Historically, gatekeepers were slaves that were allowed in the backdoor of the slave master's plantation home, where they were given leftover food and hand-me-down clothes in return for keeping the other slaves in line and informing the slave master of any escape plans or revolts. They were taught to be subservient to the slave master and brainwashed to believe that slavery was hereditary.

Modern-day gatekeepers are found in all industry sectors. Specifically, in the education sector, gatekeepers have elite access to designated spaces where they provide oversight. Who gains access to the space is determined by them. In order to maintain the status quo, gatekeepers disallow thoughts or voices that counter the established structure. Gatekeepers, blinded by their own self-righteousness and personal desire to gain more power, are complicit with respect to social consciousness and deny the greater good for all.

Authentic Engagement: The True Essence of "Power With"

Contrary to the function of gatekeepers who safeguard the status quo, authentic engagement cultivates harmonious coexistence, which is the outcome of reciprocal communicative behavior (Figure 2.1).

Authentic engagement organically moves school communities from a segregationist construct to inclusive education. In particular, authentic engagement opens up new avenues of communication that are either dismissed or considered taboo in the traditional paradigm. Critical dialogue amplifies the voices of all that are served in the learning community.

Authentic engagement is a willful connection to an idea. Those engaged authentically buy into the vision, process, and product resulting from the idea. For example, in education ideas about student achievement, teacher preparation, parent involvement, and leadership advancement become powerful attractors that build mutual relationships. Authentic engagement puts the needs, interests, and concerns of students, teachers, district and school-based administrators, parents, and policymakers at the center of their own learning and liberation.

Authentic engagement serves as the engine of transformative change. This framework for effective change provides a pragmatic means for facilitating ethical change by motivating and fueling the shifting of values, assumptions, and beliefs affecting judgment toward action. Power through voice, relationship connectivity, and true collaboration ground sustainable change.

What Did We Learn in This Chapter?
A List of Key Takeaways

- ✓ Personal bias and perceptions of race, class, and culture must be acknowledged, dismantled, and reframed in order to accept and respect diverse worldviews.
- ✓ Colonial power dynamics control and oppress minority groups even though America claims to represent everyone equally.
- ✓ Massification brainwashes the dominant culture in society to live and breathe as a supreme colony among those they have classified as others.
- ✓ Gatekeepers are significant barriers to the free flow of transformative thought and moral imperatives that are critical to the systems that serve an increasingly diverse population.

Closing Reflection Questions

Directions: Consider what you have learned in this chapter as you respond to the questions below. Be aware of how new information and understandings can help you reframe your ideas and opinions.

- ✓ How is the burden of race evidenced in the educational experience of a student of color? Provide some specific examples.
- ✓ What is the impact of race on the system of education, and who does it serve?
- ✓ How does the system of education cultivate a racist ideology?

References

Akbar, N. (1996). Psychological legacy of slavery. In *Breaking the chains of psychological slavery* (pp. 1–26). Mind Productions and Associates. https://pdfcoffee.com/breaking-the-chains-of-psychological-slavery-pdf-free.html

Bell, L. A. (1997). Theoretical foundations for social justice education. In M. Adams, L. A. Bell, & P. Griffin (Eds.), *Teaching for diversity and social justice: A sourcebook* (pp. 1–15). Routledge.

Carone, T. (2019). The school to prison pipeline: Widespread disparities in school discipline based on race. *Public Interest Law Reporter*, 24(2). https://lawecommons.luc.edu/cgi/viewcontent.cgi?article=1570&context=pilr

CBS News. (2020). What children learn about African American history depends on where they live. *CBSNews.com*. https://www.cbsnews.com/video/what-children-learn-about-african-american-history-depends-on-where-they-live/#x

Clance, P. R., & Imes, S. A. (1978). The impostor phenomenon in high achieving women: Dynamics and therapeutic intervention. *Psychotherapy: Theory, Research, and Practice*, 15(3), 241–247. https://mpowir.org/wp-content/uploads/2010/02/Download-IP-in-High-Achieving-Women.pdf

Dantley, M. E. (2002). Uprooting and replacing positivism, the melting pot, multiculturalism, and other impotent notions in educational leadership through an African American perspective. *Education and Urban Society, 34*(3), 334–352.

Diversity Inc Staff. (2019). Imposter syndrome can take a heavy toll on people of color, particularly African Americans. *Diversityinc. com*. https://www.diversityinc.com/imposter-syndrome-can-take-a-heavy-toll-on-people-of-color-particularly-african-americans/

Freire, P. (1987). *Education for critical consciousness*. The Continuum Publishing Company.

Gandara, P. (2002). Meeting common goals: Linking K–12 and college interventions. In W. G. Tierney & L. S. Hagedorn (Eds.), *Increasing access to college: Extending possibilities for all students* (pp. 81–103). State University of New York Press.

Getahun, D., Jacobson, S., & Fassett, M. (2013). *Childhood diagnosis of ADHD increased dramatically over nine-year period*. Kaiser Permanente Southern California Department of Research & Evaluation. https://www.kp-scalresearch.org/childhood-diagnosis-of-adhd-increased-dramatically-over-nine-year-period/

Gordon, N. (2018). *Disproportionality in student discipline: Connecting policy to research*. Brookings Institution. https://www.brookings.edu/research/disproportionality-in-student-discipline-connecting-policy-to-research/

Howard, T. (2003). A tug of war for our minds: African American high school students' perceptions of their academic identities and college aspirations. *The High School Journal, 87*(1), 4–17.

Johnson, U. (2013). *Psycho-academic holocaust: The special education & ADHD wars against Black boys*. Prince of Pan-Africanism Publishing.

Lynch, M. (2018, February 1). What you need to know about the school to prison pipeline. *The Edvocate*. https://www.theedadvocate.org/need-know-school-prison-pipeline/#:~:text=Unfortunately%2C%20an%20increasing%20number%20of,%2Dto%2Dprison%20pipeline.%E2%80%9D

McCluney, C., Robotham, K., Lee, S., Smith, R., & Durkee, M. (2019, November 15). The costs of code-switching. *Harvard Business Review*. https://hbr.org/2019/11/the-costs-of-codeswitching

McLaren, P. L., & Dantley, M. (1990). Leadership and a critical pedagogy of race: Cornel West, Stuart Hall, and the prophetic tradition. *The Journal of Negro Education, 59*(1), 29–44.

Okonofua, J. A., & Eberhardt, J. L. (2105). Two strikes: Race and the disciplining of young students. *Psychological Science, 26*(5), 617–624.

Pearman, F. (2020). *Anti-Blackness and the way forward for K–12 schooling.* Brookings Institution. https://www. brookings.edu/blog/brown-center-chalkboard/2020/07/01/ anti-blackness-and-the-way-forward-for-k-12-schooling/amp/

Piedra, A. (2018, February 1). *The tragedy of American education: The role of John Dewey.* The Institute of World Politics. https:// www.iwp.edu/articles/2018/02/01/the-tragedy-of-american-education-the-role-of-john-dewey/

Riddle, T., & Sinclair, S. (2019, April 2). Racial disparities in school-based disciplinary actions are associated with count-level rates of racial bias. *Proceedings of the National Academy of Sciences, 116*(17). https://www.pnas.org/doi/10.1073/pnas.1808307116

Silverman, D. (2022, August 17). 3 steps teachers can take to value students' marginalized identities. Edweek.org. https://www. edweek.org/teaching-learning/opinion-3-steps-teachers-can-take-to-value-students-marginalized-identities/2022/08

Takyi-Micah, N. (2021). *The devaluation of oneself: Dealing with imposter syndrome in the Black community.* Communitysolutions. com. https://www.communitysolutions.com/devaluation-oneself-dealing-imposter-syndrome-black-community/

Additional Reading

Carver-Madalon, L. (2018). *You belong in the room—Exploring impostor syndrome from a Black perspective.* Maryville University. https://online.maryville.edu/blog/impostor-syndrome-black-perspective/

Cronin, T. (1987). Leadership and democracy. In J. T. Wren (Ed.), *The leader's companion* (pp. 303–309). The Free Press.

The Edvocate. (2017). Black boys in crisis: Eliminating the school-to-prison pipeline. https://www.theedadvocate.org/black-boys-crisis-eliminating-school-prison-pipeline/

Larson, C. L., & Murtadha, K. (2002). Leadership for social justice. In J. Murphy (Ed.), *The educational leadership challenge: Redefining leadership for the 21st century* (pp. 134–161). Chicago: University of Chicago Press.

Parlakian, R., & Sanchez, S. (2006). *Cultural influences on early language and literacy teaching practices*. Potts Family Foundation. http://pottsfamilyfoundation.org/wp-content/uploads/2010/09/ZTT27-1_Parlakian1.pdf

PBS News. (2022). Black History Month: How new rules are limiting diversity education in schools. *PBS Newshour*. https://www.pbs.org/newshour/show/black-history-month-how-new-rules-are-limiting-diversity-education-in-schools

Villaseñor, P. (2019). *The different ways that teachers can influence the socio-emotional development of their students: A literature review*. worldbank.org. https://thedocs.worldbank.org/en/doc/285491571864192787-0050022019/original/VillasenoThedifferentwaysthatteacherscaninfluencethesocioemotionaldevofstudents.pdf

West, C. (1994). *Race matters*. Random House.

CHAPTER 3

Examining Personal Bias and Privilege Through Self-Reflection

It is very difficult to give up our certainties—our positions, our beliefs, our explanations. These help define us; they lie at the heart of our personal identity. Yet, I believe we will succeed in changing this world only if we can think and work together in new ways.

Curiosity is what we need. We don't have to let go of what we believe, but we do need to be curious about what someone else believes. We do need to acknowledge that their way of interpreting the world might be essential to our survival.

—Margaret Wheatley

Introduction

According to American doctrine, education is the great equalizer that allows all sectors of the citizenry access to full participation in society. This ideology, although laudable, is the root of one of America's greatest paradoxes. The institution of education is structured to track students and group them according to ability and skills. Social constructs of race, culture, and socioeconomic status influence the classification of historically marginalized students in schools. Recognizing that colonialist principles and norms reflect prejudice, stereotyping, and cultural ignorance, this chapter will expose the conscious and unconscious practices of White dominance and privilege through self-reflection and analysis of a real-world scenario.

Opening Reflection Questions

Directions: Before reading the chapter, take a few minutes to reflect on and respond to each of the questions below. These questions will help you become aware of your own perspectives, opinions, and experiences.

1. What advantages have you experienced as a result of your race or ethnicity?
2. What disadvantages have you experienced as a result of your race or ethnicity?
3. Have you ever witnessed what you thought might be an example of someone exerting privilege? If so, reflect on what you witnessed and how the experience made you feel. Did the experience prompt you to act or speak? Explain.
4. What are the implications of racial belonging in schools?

MR. CURCIO'S STORY*

Saintville High School (SHS) is the hallmark of academic excellence. As a blue-ribbon school, SHS distinguishes itself as a cut above the rest academically. The sports program also touts division championships for field hockey and soccer. Mr. Curcio, the principal of Saintville, was born and raised in the town. His father is the former high school football coach, and his mother teaches at Danser Elementary, one of the two elementary schools in town.

A developer bought the farmland that borders Saintville. Luxury housing and commercial businesses were constructed. Subsidized housing units were also built. Since the architectural design and number of low-income housing units included in the design met township requirements, the township council approved the plan.

As new families began to move in, the residents of Saintville started to notice some changes in their community. The texture of the community was "tainted." The traditional smells, sounds, and look of Saintville were in transition. At one township meeting, a resident publicly proclaimed that Saintville was beginning to look like Liberty, the community located on the other side of the railroad tracks.

As students from the new housing development enrolled at SHS, Mr. Curcio observed and felt some changes in the dispositions of the teachers and staff. He also noticed that student assessment scores had dropped. As he conducted a deep review of the data, he identified that most of the students fell into one or more sub-groups. The harsh reality was that most were new enrollments; the students who lived in the newly constructed subsidized housing.

Mr. Curcio knew what the community members were saying about the new families. He himself was ambushed in the supermarket, parking lots, and even at church by residents who felt the need to cast aspersions and express their dissatisfaction. He knew that new faces in the community usually caused some gossip and cattiness, but this was different. The fiery uproar in the community alarmed him!

*The vignette is based on a real-world experience of one of the authors.

Historical Ruptures: White Privilege and Entitlement

To act is to be committed, and to be committed is to be in danger. In this case, the danger, in the minds of most white Americans, is the loss of their identity.

—James Baldwin

White Privilege

Since encroaching on the land of the Indigenous peoples of the Western hemisphere, European settlers have sought to maintain their dominance and power by employing principles of colonialism (Collins, 2018). European colonialism has provided the foundation for White privilege that continues to exist today in every corner of American society. White privilege is a sense of entitlement that is ingrained in the mindset of Euro-American citizens from childhood, which in turn fuels adult norms (Collins, 2018). The distinction of privilege is often unrecognizable to most Whites because there is no need for them to strive for acceptance and belonging (Mirken, 2015).

History dictates that White women have been a symbol of entitlement and false narratives by accusing Black males of crimes that they did not commit. Emmett Till, the Scottsboro Boys, and many other Black males were murdered or convicted because of false accusations by White women (Selby, 2020). In 1921, Sarah Page, an elevator operator in Tulsa, Oklahoma, falsely accused Dick Rowland of sexually assaulting her. The false accusation by Page was the catalyst of one of the worst race massacres in U.S. history, better known as the Tulsa Massacre (History.com Editors, 2022). As a result, angry Whites rampaged through what was a thriving Black neighborhood in the Greenwood section of the city, better known as Black Wall Street, and claimed the lives of hundreds of residents, burned down over 1,200 homes, and destroyed nearly 200 Black businesses (History.com Editors, 2022).

Some White women continue to exert the power from their legacy of entitlement by policing Blacks in public places. This is called "the Karen effect" (Schmitt, 2021). "Karen" is the pejorative used for a demanding, entitled White woman (Phelps-Roper, 2021). In 2020, a White woman named Amy Cooper falsely accused Christian Cooper (no relation), a Black man, of threatening her and her dog while she was walking in Central Park. Fortunately, Christian recorded the conversation between the two on his cellphone. Amy Cooper was later charged and received consequences for falsely reporting the incident to the police. Amy Cooper's weaponization of White tears earned her the name "The Central Park Karen." In 2021, Miya

Ponsetto verbally assaulted and tackled Keyon Harrold Jr., a fourteen-year-old Black teenager, at a New York City hotel. She wrongly accused him of stealing her cellphone, which was later found in the Uber she hired (Shanahan, 2022). This incident earned her the name "SoHo Karen."

Self-Identity and a Sense of Belonging

America's historical ruptures and centuries-old Eurocentric ideologies undergird today's system of racial inequality. Racialized fear, evidenced through "Karen" practices, continues to perpetuate systemic racism. The power over dynamic (Figure 2.2), discussed in Chapter 2, emphasizes the power differential that points to White superiority.

Community and public space must contain environmental conditions that are conducive for participants to authentically engage in collaboration. The community makeup encourages individual realities to coexist. Community norms are the foundation of reciprocal communicative behavior (Figure 2.1). Specifically, the norms are agreements among all participants in the community. They provide a framework for actions, behaviors, and interactions within the community. Critical to successful coexistence within community is the willingness of all community members to acknowledge, respect, and empower each other to voice their thoughts, beliefs, and views. As the community grows, negotiating individual realities becomes more complex.

Lifeworlds: Our Metaverse of Personal Norms

Brookfield (2005) describes a lifeworld as being pervasive; unconsciously existing and functioning as a background in our life. A visual is that of a massive data cloud saturated with terabytes of information positioned to be accessed and used at a moment's notice. One's limited bandwidth of life experiences populates the database and algorithms are coded based on personal norms. This source provides a constant data feed into our objective world and our worldviews are cultivated by our lifeworld data, whether we are aware of its presence or not. Brookfield adds that our lifeworld saturates our conversations with cultural knowledge that is familiar and comfortable to us.

The lifeworld is important for comprehending how we engage in community. Over time, our lifeworld frames our thoughts, attitudes, and behaviors. These regularities become subconscious and surface when there is a disturbance in the social system. For example, in looking at the opening vignette, we see that the introduction of diverse families to Saintville represents such a disturbance. The impact of the disturbance is outgroup bias, implied by the behaviors and actions of community members. Outgroup bias is the psychological tendency to dislike individuals who are outside of one's identity group, which undermines the ability to be open to, welcome, or include anyone who is not part of the in-group (Cherry, 2020).

There are two acclaimed psychological experiments that investigated bias mindsets. Jane Elliott's blue eyes–brown eyes exercise challenged the lifeworld perceptions of third-grade students. In the 1960s schoolteacher Jane Elliott split her third-grade class by eye color. The first day, she named the blue-eyed group as superior and the brown-eyed group as inferior. The blue-eyed group was praised and validated while the brown-eyed group received negative remarks and comments. Later, the roles of the groups were switched. While the objective of the exercise was to teach students about the effects of racism, it became known nationwide as a study of outgroup bias (Bland, 2017).

The Stanford Prison Experiment (1971) is a notorious simulation study on the psychology of imprisonment. Over a two-week period, twenty-four college-age men, recruited from the local community, were assigned the role of either prisoner or guard. The participants who were selected to be guards were given guard uniforms and permission to act with authority. The "prisoners" were arrested by the police, then incarcerated. They were treated brutally by the guards. The dehumanization illustrated the ease with which individuals could be led to engage in antisocial acts when they perceive others as outliers or inferior. The experiment was canceled after the first week due to acts of revolt against the guards and fear of psychological trauma of the participants (Zimbardo, n.d.).

Outgroup bias can clearly lead to volatile and severe consequences. The conscious or unconscious assumptions about certain identified groups that are not part of the favored group activates fear, anxieties, and misjudgments that will lead to the exclusion and polarization of "others" who are not part of the in-group (Cherry, 2020).

Communicative Action

Communicative action is central to nurturing reciprocal relationships in the community. Communicative action expresses a mindset of community that coalesces around a given interest. When those in the community willingly and purposely bring their perspectives together to address a situation, circumstance, or challenge of any kind, they are able to holistically develop corresponding concrete structures. In other words, they co-construct an environment that fosters fairness and equity. Participating in community to reach a common, agreed-upon goal through nonstrategic processes is the organic, selfless process that provokes the authentic engagement required to create learning spaces that meet the needs of all learners.

STOP, THINK, AND REFLECT

Consider that each of us has a lifeworld we bring with us wherever we go. What experiences might be logged within your lifeworld as you move about addressing topics in various situations? To reveal a sample of what may be present for you, take a moment to complete the following activity.

Write three words that described a *good student* when you were in grade school.

1. _____ 2. _____ 3. _____

Study your list carefully. Now consider the following prompts:

- Are you surprised by what descriptors emerged?
- How do the descriptors you listed affect your view of the students you serve?
- Do any of the words you listed accurately describe students in your classroom or school today?
- Furthermore, is it appropriate to frame all students with your perception of a "good student"?

What is most important about this exercise is that you come to recognize the data deposited in your lifeworld experience and that it surfaces when you initiate the process of interpretation to address a situation. You use any and all data stored about *the good student* to frame your relationships with all students. In fact, closer scrutiny on your part may reveal how the stored descriptions are used to shape your assumptions about all students.

Othering: The Juncture of Misperceptions and Reality

Returning to the opening vignette, the scenario reveals that Saintville community members are not naturally oriented toward accepting all the new families. As stated, "At one township meeting, a resident publicly proclaimed that Saintville was beginning to look like Liberty, the community located on the other side of the railroad tracks." Railroad tracks are a historic demarcation of socioeconomic status (SES). Accordingly, the idiom suggests that the Saintville community is beginning to take on the characteristics of its neighbor, Liberty, where low-SES families reside. Further, as the new, diverse families in Saintville are being defined and labeled as outsiders, biased social identification and community belonging emerge.

Attributing negative qualities to groups that are different from you signals *othering*. Othering is the antithesis of belonging. Where belonging suggests acceptance and inclusion of all individuals, othering implies intolerance and exclusion. Accordingly, the feeling of alarm that the comments of the Saintville community members evoked in Mr. Curcio unmasked stereotypes and bias that he had never experienced in his community. Surprised by the manifestation of the us versus them dynamic, he knew that introducing the students from these new families to Saintville High School would be a social change that he did not look forward to leading.

Grappling With Unapologetic Discomfort

Overseers in the education space, who knowingly or unknowingly exert White privilege, have taken Blacks from physical bondage to psychological bondage by conveying false narratives for the purpose of maintaining power and control. Their reluctance to learn and understand the cultural identity of people from diverse backgrounds distorts the essence of authentic communication and creates barriers to progression. To address critical communicative action, it is important to examine the process of effective intercultural communication and its impact. Lustig and Koester (2013) describe intercultural communication as a two-way process in which people from different cultures create shared meanings of communication that allow both speaker and listener to understand each other regardless of their culture (Figure 2.1).

Historian Carter G. Woodson's critique of the miseducation of Blacks maintains that Black education is developed through a series of handicaps, including state-sanctioned actions that undermined and blocked attempts at Black educational progress. Woodson went on to say "that to handicap a student by teaching him that his black face is a curse and that his struggle to change his condition is hopeless is the worst sort of lynching. It kills one's aspirations and dooms him to vagabondage and crime" (1933, p. 3). His statement is reflective of the present state of marginalized students in public education in the United States, which can only be changed if the overseers of education are committed to dismantling a system that bears resemblance to its origin of exclusivity and White dominance.

White teachers and educational leaders, who are changemakers, will inhabit unfamiliar spaces as advocates for inclusive education. The courage to confront feelings of White guilt, which is the psychosocial consequence of racism, is a prerequisite to engagement in critical conversation that addresses the historical underpinnings of race, class, and culture in American education. Discourse ethics opens up the space for diverse and co-created constructivist thoughts. Specifically, discourse ethics "confines itself to the limited task of reconstructing the moral point of view, leaving concrete moral and ethical judgments to all participants" (Habermas, 1991, p. xi). In other words, the freedom and equality of all allows universally valid norms to emerge. In a community that seeks to establish norms, everyone's interests are represented as a true consensus. Consensus can only be achieved if all members are welcomed to freely dialogue in such a way that the reciprocity of giving and receiving is the universal standard for all community members (Habermas, 1991).

Central to critical dialogue is self-reckoning. Honest self-reckoning positions us to face the truth about ourselves. There is a need for all individuals to be receptive to understanding the verbal and nonverbal barriers to communication that prevent healthy intercultural communication (Pilgrim, 2000). Meaningful conversation about the ruptures of race, culture, and class commences when White people listen, hear, and value the voices and experiences of those who have been silenced and historically excluded from the educational process and intuitively search within themselves to identify corrupt values that anchor and stimulate beliefs of White dominance.

Assimilation Reconnaissance

A founding principle of America is the idea of individual freedom. The historical precedence and persistent endurance of injustice in the nation continues to host and placate societal norms that endorse out-group bias and the dehumanization of marginalized groups. Systemic bias challenges fairness and virtue in humanity's pursuit of improving intercultural communication and constructing social institutions. America's institutions of learning profile students of color through the lens of the injustices that are woven into the fabric of America. Low-end tracking and ability grouping, discipline disproportionality, and the overidentification of students of color for special education are a few examples of the mechanisms of oppression in education.

The American education system has regurgitated generation after generation of Black, Brown, and Indigenous American students who question who they are and their rightful place in society. The data shared regarding the school-to-prison pipeline in Chapter 2 represents modern-day segregation. The outlook for historically marginalized students is bleak when statistics indicate that 70% of all in-school arrests are of Black and Brown students (Lynch, 2018). Accordingly, hope for these students quickly fades as their life trajectory abruptly changes course from being a students in school to numbers in the penal system.

Othering has a devastating and harmful impact on students, who are plagued with self-hate, low self-confidence, and poor self-esteem. Specifically, students of color directly link their academic identity to their cultural identity. Typecasting by their name, what they look like, as well as where and how they live compromises a student's sense of belonging and possibility of acceptance in school. The apparent achievement disparity between Black and Brown students and their White counterparts is an alarming result of systematically minoritized populations struggling under the weight of the tradition of marginalization.

What Did We Learn in This Chapter?
A List of Key Takeaways

✓ White privilege and entitlement are rooted in the Eurocentric ideologies of America.

✓ Our lifeworld reflects our personal perceptions, realities, and beliefs, which in turn influence our attitudes and behaviors toward diverse races and cultural groups.

✓ For historically marginalized students, othering is detrimental to their existence, survival, development, and success.

✓ Cultural responsiveness is critical to inclusive teaching and learning, and cultural proficiency, as a mindset and practice, is essential to the development of safe and nurturing learning spaces for all students.

Closing Reflection Exercise

Directions: Consider what you have learned in this chapter as you complete the exercise below. Be aware of how new information and understandings can help you reframe your ideas and opinions.

Assess your need to shift personal norms in order to welcome new understandings about diverse cultures.

Self-Reflection Exercise:

- ✓ What are your perceptions of the social construct of "haves" and "have nots"? Make a list of descriptors for each construct.
- ✓ Examine your two lists and note ideas that stand out. Do any of your views surprise you? If so, take a moment to deeply examine the reasons why you were surprised.
- ✓ Compare your thoughts of the "haves" and "have nots" with the themes and content in Chapters 1–3.
- ✓ Will you be shifting your personal norms?

References

Bland, K. (2017, November 17). Blue eyes, brown eyes: What Jane Elliott's famous experiment says about race 50 years on. *The Republic.* https://www.azcentral.com/story/news/local/karinabland/2017/11/17/blue-eyes-brown-eyes-jane-elliotts-exercise-race-50-years-later/860287001/

Brookfield, S. D. (2005). *The power of critical theory: Liberating adult learning and teaching.* Jossey-Bass.

Cherry, K. (2020, December 13). What is othering? *VeryWellMind.* https://www.verywellmind.com/what-is-othering-5084425#:~:text=Othering%20is%20a%20way%20of,prejudices%20against%20people%20and%20groups

Collins, C. (2018). *What is White privilege, really?* learningforjustice.org. https://www.learningforjustice.org/magazine/fall-2018/what-is-white-privilege-really

Habermas, J. (1991). *Moral consciousness and communicative action.* MIT Press.

History.com Editors. (2022). *Tulsa race massacre.* History.com. https://www.history.com/topics/roaring-twenties/tulsa-race-massacre

Lustig, M., & Koester, J. (2013). *Intercultural competence* (7th ed.). Pearson.

Lynch, M. (2018, February 1). What you need to know about the school to prison pipeline. *The Advocate.* https://www.theedadvocate.org/need-know-school-prison-pipeline/

Mirken, B. (2015, July). A case study in White privilege. Greenlining.org. https://greenlining.org/blog-category/2015/a-case-study-in-white-privilege/?gclid=EAIaIQobChMItIvNtpnX9gIVx8DICh2wdQDyEAAYBCAAEgLoBfD_BwE

Phelps-Roper, M. (2021, August 3). The real story of "The Central Park Karen." *The Free Press.* https://www.thefp.com/p/the-real-story-of-the-central-park?s=r

Pilgrim, D. (2000). *What was Jim Crow?* Jim Crow Museum. Ferris State University. https://www.ferris.edu/HTMLS/news/jimcrow/what.htm

Schmitt, C. (2021, February 3). Deconstructing the "Karen" meme. *Harvard Law Today.* https://today.law.harvard.edu/deconstructing-the-karen-meme/

Selby, D. (2020). From Emmett Till to Pervis Payne—Black men in America are still killed for crimes they didn't commit. *Innocence Project.* https://innocenceproject.org/news/emmett-till-birthday-pervis-payne-innocent-black-men-slavery-racism/

Shanahan, E. (2022, April 11). Woman pleads guilty to tackling Black teen at SoHo hotel. *New York Times,* https://www.nytimes.com/2022/04/11/nyregion/miya-ponsetto-soho-hotel-guilty-plea.html

Woodson, C. G. (1933). *The mis-education of the Negro.* The Associated Publishers.

Zimbardo, P. G. (n.d.). *Stanford prison experiment.* https://www.prisonexp.org/

Additional Reading

Ibrahim A. A., & Faisal A. A. (2019). Non-verbal barriers to effective intercultural communication. Utopía y Praxis Latinoamericana, 24(5), 307–316. https://www.redalyc.org/journal/279/27962050034/html/

McIntosh, P. (1989). *White privilege: Unpacking the invisible knapsack and some notes for facilitators.* National Seed Project. https://nationalseedproject.org/Key-SEED-Texts/white-privilege-unpacking-the-invisible-knapsack

Monroe, A. (2006). *Co-creation: Shifting the source of policy-making power* [Unpublished doctoral dissertation]. Rowan University.

The Opportunity Agenda. (2011). *Media representations and impact on the lives of Black men and boys: A social science literature review.* https://opportunityagenda.org/messaging_reports/media-representations-black-men-boys/

Wheatley, M. J. (2002). *Turning to one another: Simple conversations to restore hope to the future.* Berrett-Koehler Publishers.

CHAPTER 4

Unshackling the Silenced Voice

... and when we speak we are afraid

our words will not be heard

nor welcomed

but when we are silent

we are still afraid

So it is better to speak

remembering

we were never meant to survive

—Audre Lorde

Introduction

Cultural differences are rich with various customs, traditions, beliefs, and values that can provide a better understanding of the social and emotional behaviors of people from diverse backgrounds. This chapter will take a deep look at personal identity and will spotlight voice empowerment as critical to the liberation and freedom of marginalized groups. An original framework designed for the creation of authentically engaged community space will be introduced and unpacked.

Opening Reflection Exercise

Directions: Before reading the chapter, take a few minutes to complete the exercise below. The exercise will help you become aware of your own perspectives, opinions, and experiences.

Who are you? List 5 descriptors of your identity (i.e., race, ethnicity, culture, class, gender, sexual orientation, ability, religion/spirituality, nationality, etc.).

1. Of the descriptors that you identified, select 3 that you closely associate with.
2. Identify the descriptor that is your primary identifier. Eliminate the other 2 descriptors. How does it make you feel to relinquish all but one of your descriptors? Explain the reasons for your feelings.
3. After you've completed the elimination of all but one of your descriptors, share your descriptor with a partner.
4. Ask your partner to name 4 descriptors that they feel identify you (i.e., race, ethnicity, culture, class, gender, sexual orientation, ability, religion/spirituality, nationality, etc.). There should be no input from you during your partner's selection process.
5. Take a moment to self-reflect. Compare the descriptors that you identified for yourself to those that your partner selected.
6. Now, imagine your partner's 4 descriptors in addition to your 1 define your personal narrative. What emotions are evoked within you by having someone else tell your story?

ESPERANZA'S STORY*

Esperanza Ruiz is a senior at New Jersey State College (NJSC). She entered NJSC through the Educational Opportunity Fund (EOF) program and is a stellar student. Esperanza regularly met with her EOF counselor, Ms. Jenkins (who is African American), and participated in events throughout her freshman year. Esperanza and her EOF counselor have a wonderful rapport and developed a great relationship over the year. Her friends would often joke with her, saying, "When you are looking for Esperanza, look in the EOF suite first."

At the start of her sophomore year, Esperanza learned that Ms. Jenkins was no longer at the college. As a result, she was assigned a new EOF counselor who was recently hired—Ms. McIntyre, who is White. After her first three visits, Esperanza felt that the possibility of developing a meaningful connection with Ms. McIntyre was slim to none. Several times Ms. McIntyre asked Esperanza how to correctly pronounce her name. Nevertheless, she continued to butcher it. Instead of learning the correct pronunciation of her name, she said to Esperanza "Since I can't seem to figure out how to pronounce your name, I will call you 'Hope.'" For Esperanza, this was the tipping point. Not only were the visits to Ms. McIntyre cold, quick, and very routine, she didn't even care enough to learn the correct pronunciation of Esperanza's name. Esperanza refused to be called Hope, which is the English version of her name. She is of a legacy of strong, resilient women in her family with the same name. Consequently, Esperanza felt diminished. She concluded that meeting with Ms. McIntyre was a waste of her time. Therefore, she stopped scheduling her monthly EOF appointments.

For the first time in her three and a half years at NJSC, Esperanza was selected for financial aid verification. She decided to handle the verification process on her own because she had no relationship with Ms. McIntyre. Esperanza had been successfully self-sufficient for three years. Esperanza submitted the documents that were requested from her by the Financial Aid Office in a timely manner. Yet, when she attempted to register for classes for the spring semester, she was denied. Perplexed, Esperanza spoke with the Registrar's Office, which informed her of a $5,500 outstanding balance on her account. In despair, Esperanza went to the Financial Aid Office and was told that her Tuition Aid Grant (TAG) was not processed. She was directed to call the TAG office. When Esperanza called the TAG office, the representative informed her that her employment verification was missing. Consequently, she would not be awarded TAG funds because she missed the November 15 deadline. Since Esperanza had submitted her letter and documents to the college's Financial Aid Office on November 1, she thought that she fulfilled all of the requirements for the financial aid verification process.

Exasperated, Esperanza decided to go to the EOF Office to ask Ms. McIntyre for assistance and guidance. Ms. McIntyre sat and listened to Esperanza explain her situation. After twenty minutes, Ms. McIntyre expressed her sympathy, then informed Esperanza that there was nothing that she could do about the situation. Esperanza appealed to Ms. McIntyre for her help. In response, Ms. McIntyre replied, "Unfortunately, Esperanza, when you do not submit paperwork in a timely manner, these things happen." In response, Esperanza stormed out of the office in tears, thinking to herself, "This is my last semester. I'm the first person in my family to go to college and I'm not going to graduate! I let my family down!"

The vignette is based on a real-world experience of one of the authors.

Esperanza: The Outlook
In the vignette we meet Esperanza Ruiz, a first-generation college student whose parents are naturalized citizens. Her ethnic identity is Latinx. Nonetheless, through developing a relationship with Esperanza, one of the authors learned that she identifies with several marginalized groups.

Ms. McIntyre's attitude and practice of cultural destructiveness, along with her lack of empathy, instigated the downward spiral in her communication with Esperanza. We learn that the counseling visits were "quick, cold, and very routine." It can also be surmised that Ms. McIntyre did not convey her value for Esperanza, since she was not committed to learning the correct pronunciation of her name. In addition, she felt entitled to change Esperanza's name to "Hope" because it was simpler and more convenient for her. When Esperanza asked for help from Ms. McIntyre three and a half years later, Ms. McIntyre gave Esperanza twenty minutes of her time and didn't provide her with any assistance or support. Disturbingly, Ms. McIntyre is described as sympathetic, which suggests that she viewed Esperanza's problem through a deficit lens. Accordingly, her worldviews framed her dismissive response: "Unfortunately, Esperanza, when you do not submit paperwork in a timely manner, these things happen."

All forms of inequality are directly tied to oppression. Intersectionality demonstrates that a combination of social identities result in unique experiences that can provide opportunities or barriers for a person (The University of British Columbia, 2021). To understand intersectionality, individuals must reflect on their own identities and intersections and be willing to deepen their understanding of the intersection of identities and power structures that impact marginalized groups (The University of British Columbia, 2021). In this case, Ms. McIntyre is a gatekeeper whose interwoven biases and privilege prevented her from developing a relationship with Esperanza. As a result, Esperanza did not receive the guidance, support, empathy, and access to resources that were critical to her academic success.

American Pluralism and Cultural Proficiency

Schools reflect the inequality embedded in the frame of our country. However, the changing face of America demands a new approach to inclusion. The concept of the melting pot has been replaced by the notion of cultural pluralism, which calls for an understanding and appreciation of the cultural values of diverse groups (Orlando et al., 2003). Cultural pluralism promotes a mosaic in which each sub-group maintains its own individuality but combines to make our society a unique whole (Orlando et al., 2003). Schools that embrace cultural pluralism seek to promote diversity and avoid Eurocentric dominance.

Cultural proficiency is a way of being that enables individuals to effectively respond to individuals unlike themselves (Lindsey et al., 2005). An acceptable approach to cultural proficiency is designed to reflect the environment in which it exists. The setting gives cultural proficiency the foundation for shifting the culture. Allowing the model for organizational change to be established inside schools supports the position that the transformation of American education must and can only come from within.

To be human is to engage in relationships with others and the world (Freire, 1987; Maturana & Varela, 1987). As "cultural proficiency requires understanding and mastery of the modes of conversation that promote effective communication" (Lindsey et al., 2005, p. 129), examining one's own beliefs and values enables an individual to better understand the impact their beliefs and actions have on others. Achieving cultural proficiency involves building a safe environment where individuals feel comfortable engaging in dialogue regarding their beliefs, values, and perceptions. Healthy conditions for change are cultivated when individuals begin to trust each other and fully invest in the process.

Changemakers embody the qualities that facilitate movement toward cultural proficiency. Within this context, transformative leaders must have the vision and the genuine spirit to inspire true dialogue and ultimately the creation of a shared vision and the development of a strong collective culture. Culturally proficient leaders walk the talk. They take responsibility for their own learning, have a vision for what education should be like for all students, effectively share the vision, assess their personal beliefs and values, and understand the structural and organic nature of schools (Lindsey et al., 2003). Stakeholders from various sectors influence the education system. Although tradition dictates that change comes from inside the education system, external stakeholders can also impact the change process.

Framing and Reframing: A Constructive Approach to Conflict

The recursive process of framing and reframing is critical to conflict resolution (Putnam & Holmer, 1992). Since disputants have mental models that differ in significant ways, framing and reframing diverse worldviews drives dialogue toward resolution (Kaufman et al., 2003). When examining the process of framing and reframing, we must first view each position separately and identify its purpose in resolving conflict.

Reframing is a process that involves the clarification of differences, reconciliation, and problem-solving with all participants for the purpose of finding communality (Kaufman et al., 2003). The reframing process involves accessing independent views, tapping into personal biases and traditions, and acquiring a better understanding of different views. Reframing affords participants the opportunity to modify their viewpoints. More importantly, the process activates the silent voice. All voices are liberated and free to speak, be heard, and be active in the advancement of resolution and healing.

Upon deeper examination of the opening vignette, it is clear that the onus was on Ms. McIntyre to develop a relationship with Esperanza. Through reframing the initial meetings with Esperanza, if Ms. McIntyre "spoke with" instead of "spoke at" Esperanza, she would lay the foundation of reciprocal communicative behavior (Figure 2.1). Polite conversation with Esperanza would have provided opportunities for Ms. McIntyre to uncover meaningful content about her personal identity, her family history, and her academic goals and objectives, which are data needed to create a healthy counseling space. In addition, Ms. McIntyre would also be sharing information about herself during their exchange. As healthy rapport evolved, Esperanza would begin to trust Ms. McIntyre and develop a sense of belonging.

Accountability Is Reciprocal

Disenfranchisement of minoritized groups stems from resistance to change by Euro-Americans. Euro-Americans fear that their power and privilege will be dismantled, so mechanisms for negotiation are unfathomable. If reaching common ground is the purpose, it is imperative that we create frames to help us understand why the conflict exists, what actions are important to the conflict, why the parties act as they do, and how we should act in response (Putnam & Holmer, 1992).

With a focus on education, shared accountability and reciprocal accountability are essential for creating a learning environment that is inclusive and receptive to voices from diverse backgrounds. Currently, the blatant disparities between the educational experiences of historically marginalized students and their White counterparts signal the absence of both. Shared accountability means that internal and external stakeholders have a "seat at the table" and are equally held accountable to support high-quality education for all students. Reciprocal accountability means that if educational leaders are going to hold teachers accountable, then those leaders have an equal responsibility to ensure that teachers know how to do what is expected of them. Reciprocal accountability and organizational capacity-building must work in tandem in order for teachers to have the expertise needed to support high achievement for all students (Fink, 2014).

Defining ALL as Every = Each

- **All** refers to the whole quantity.
- **Every** refers to all the individual members of a set, without exception.
- **Each** refers to every one of two or more people or things, regarded and identified separately.

The terms *all*, *every*, and *each* imply inclusion. They similarly refer to whole quantities and connote connection. In a learning community that is inclusive and receptive of all students, every participant in the community shares the responsibility of providing a high-quality education for each student.

Educators are uniquely positioned to develop relationships with their students. Studies reveal that positive student–teacher relationships boost students' academic development and sense of belonging (Arundel, 2022). The opening vignette clearly demonstrates the impact of positive and negative student–educator relationships. Trust and safety are fundamental needs for historically marginalized students. Esperanza, in connection with Ms. Jenkins, thrived her freshman year of college. However, she felt disenfranchised by Ms. McIntyre, and therefore disconnected with her at the beginning of her sophomore year. By legitimately creating space and providing opportunities for all students to succeed there is a reciprocal benefit. In correlation with the increase in student achievement and belonging, positive student–teacher relationships also impact effective instructional practices, engagement, and student retention.

The Authentically Engaged Community

According to Maslow's Hierarchy of Needs (Maslow, 2017), which classifies human motivation, individuals need food, water, and shelter; to feel safe and secure; and to have a sense of belonging in order to holistically participate in community. Educators can successfully establish a learning community that nurtures student motivation. The classroom is a teacher's space to develop a culture of achievement and belonging for all students. Of equal importance, educators working together to understand and address the needs of all students as well as those of their fellow educators yield an educational ecosystem where both students and educators thrive.

The authentically engaged community is a dialogic community in which the essential environmental conditions of safety, trust, acceptance, respect, the empowerment of every voice, and forgiveness are present and processed through a lens of empathy to achieve co-created and shared meaning. Translating the authentically engaged community framework (Figure 4.1) to learning spaces establishes that "ME" and "OTHERS" unite to create shared meaning for the students, families, educators, and stakeholders who coexist in the social system. More specifically, "ME" and the "OTHERS" must connect and negotiate norms for the learning community that inspire and sustain a shared meaning that encourages student academic and social success. The "ME" represents our story, our personal values, beliefs, and lifeworlds that are the essence of our identity, and the "OTHERS" are humans in the community. The humans that we connect with constitute the social systems that become our family, our "village," our "tribe." Human social systems form a patterned network of relationships.

The Authentically Engaged Community

There is a level of commitment that affirms confidence for ALL within the community, so as to ensure a successful community.

FIGURE 4.1 Diagram of the Authentically Engaged Community

The desire to communicate skillfully with others evolves from an individual's confidence with their personal truth and their esteem in the community in which they exist. The community makeup encourages participants to authentically engage in collaboration. Those engaged authentically trust and feel safe in the community. Accordingly, they are predisposed to voice their thoughts and comfortably engage in critical dialogue.

A community must contain environmental conditions conducive to authentic engagement. The community makeup encourages individual realities (our personal values, attitudes, and beliefs) to coexist. According to Habermas (1991), Freire (1987), Maturana and Varela (1987), and Monroe (2006), safety, trust, acceptance, respect, the empowerment of every voice, forgiveness, and empathy are required norms for a community that seeks to establish shared meaning.

Shared meaning is the core of an authentically engaged community. Conceptually, to achieve shared meaning suggests that community members either share a common language or there is a common acceptance that words can be used differently, and these differences are dignified and considered in conversations. At a deeper level, there is respect and safety for those members who possess different values, beliefs, and perspectives.

The norms illustrated in the authentically engaged community diagram (Figure 4.1) stabilize the community so that all participants can engage in a true collaboration of thoughts and ideas. Shared meaning does not mean that everyone has the same perspectives. Instead, it establishes a safe space for diverse thoughts and legitimizes all perspectives as the community is co-created.

The Environmental Conditions of an Authentically Engaged Community

Safety: Safety refers to the need for security and protection to remain safe from any harm. When safety needs of humans are met, a natural desire for a well-balanced life and order is readily achievable (Maslow, 2017).

Trust: Trust is an assured confidence in or reliance on something or someone. Trust anchors relationships among and between members in community and social systems (Maturana & Varela, 1987).

Acceptance: Acceptance is a social imperative of humanness, since we only have a world that we create with others. The acceptance of others opens up room within us for the existence of another. Acceptance leads to operational coherences in social systems (Maturana & Varela, 1987).

Respect: Respect is a deep esteem and acceptance of an individual for who they are and their abilities, qualities, and achievements, even if they are different from you or they have different thoughts, beliefs, and perspectives. Respect acknowledges identity, cultural background, intersectionality, lifeworlds, living conditions, and the importance of knowledge derived from life experiences (Freire, 2002).

The Empowerment of Every Voice: Voices are integral to the self-sustaining processes that humans embody. Human emancipation advances when all the members of a community are free to participate in critical dialogue regarding community norms and procedures. The empowerment of every voice liberates all community members to have an equal voice in the consensus that emerges from the meshing of lifeworlds. Conversely, disallowing members of the social system to equally participate in the process that defines their existence restrains the human condition (Habermas, 1991).

Forgiveness: Forgiveness is a deliberate decision to release negative emotions toward yourself or another person. Forgiveness is for healing deep wounds. Forgiveness does not necessarily come easy, but it is possible to achieve. As humans surrender negative emotions, we are healed and liberated. Forgiveness is a process with many steps that allows us to move on in life with meaning and purpose (Enright, 2015).

Empathy: Empathy is the ability to understand others' emotions. Specifically, empathy is about defining, understanding, and reacting to concerns and needs that undergird others' emotional responses and reactions as if you are experiencing them yourself. Our own emotional intelligence sensitizes us to recognize and manage our own emotions and the emotions of others (Goleman, 2007).

As educators work together to develop communicative competence, their personal realities, which depict the culture and traditions that they embrace, form a context for reaching shared meaning. In an attempt to grow, nurture, and sustain the learning community, all members are thrust into dialogue with each other. Establishing an authentically engaged community is an organic process, in which individuals position themselves to build healthy relationships in the community.

Our beliefs, attitudes, and actions lie at the heart of our identity. Thus, it is difficult to give up these certainties in order to acknowledge others and their ways of interpreting the world. In order to see, feel, and hear equity in our schools and on our campuses, we must think and work together in new ways. As schools become increasingly more diverse, we must honestly confront the barriers to achieving educational equity.

What Did We Learn in This Chapter?
A List of Key Takeaways

- ✓ Self-reflection allows us to gain perspective on who we are and to better understand the impact of our attitudes, beliefs, and actions on others.
- ✓ Dialogue creates a state of critical consciousness that advances the goals of freedom and liberation for all individuals to actively participate in community.
- ✓ Human emancipation advances when all members of the community are free to participate in critical dialogue.
- ✓ Human relationships are integral to authentic engagement and the development of a thriving learning community.

Closing Reflection Questions

Directions: Consider what you have learned in this chapter as you respond to the questions below. Be aware of how new information and understandings can help you reframe your ideas and opinions.

- ✓ What is belonging? How does belonging impact student academic and social success?
- ✓ What is cultural proficiency? What are some ways that cultural competence is measured?
- ✓ What norms are essential to maintaining and sustaining an authentically engaged community? Why are these norms necessary?

References

Arundel, K. (2022). Positive student-teacher relationships boost instructional quality. *K–12 Dive*. https://www.k12dive.com/news/teachers-benefit-from-positive-relationships-with-students-research-shows/621803/

Enright, R. (2015). Eight keys to forgiveness. *Greater Good Magazine*. https://greatergood.berkeley.edu/article/item/eight_keys_to_forgiveness

Fink, S. (2014). *Reciprocal accountability: How effective instructional leaders improve teaching and learning*. Center for Educational Leadership. University of Washington, College of Education. https://k-12leadership.org/reciprocal-accountability-how-effective-instructional-leaders-improve-teaching-and-learning/#:~:text=Simply%20stated%2C%20reciprocal%20accountability%20means%20that%20if%20school,to%20do%20what%20they%20are%20expected%20to%20do

Freire, P. (1987). *Education for critical consciousness*. The Continuum Publishing Company.

Freire, P. (2002). *Pedagogy of the oppressed* (30th ed.). The Continuum International Publishing Group, Inc.

Goleman, D. (2007). *Emotional intelligence: Why it can matter more than IQ* (10th ed.). Bantam Books.

Habermas, J. (1991). *Moral consciousness and communicative action*. MIT Press.

Kaufman, S., Elliott, M., & Shmueli, D. (2003). Frames, framing and reframing. BeyondIntractability.org. https://www.beyondintractability.org/essay/framing#narrow-body

Lindsey, R. B., Nuri-Robins, K., & Terrell, R. D. (2003). *Cultural proficiency: A manual for school leaders* (2nd ed.). Corwin Press.

Lindsey, R. B., Roberts, L. M., & CampbellJones, F. (2005). *The culturally proficient school: An implementation guide for school leaders*. Corwin Press.

Maslow, A. (2017). *A theory of human motivation*. Beta Nu Publishing. (Original work published 1943)

Maturana, H. R., & Varela, F. J. (1987). *The tree of knowledge: The biological roots of human understanding.* Shambala Publications.

Monroe, A. (2006). *Co-creation: Shifting the source of policy-making power* [Unpublished doctoral dissertation]. Rowan University.

Orlando, F. J., Levy, L. C., & Harris, J. L. (2003). *Transition to teaching* (2nd ed.). Houghton Mifflin Custom Publishing.

Putnam, L., & Holmer, M. (1992). Framing, reframing, and issue development. In L. L. Putnam & M. E. Roloff (Eds.), *Communication and negotiation* (pp. 128–155). Sage.

Schwartz, S. (2019). Teachers Push for Books with More Diversity, Fewer Stereotypes. *Edweek.org.* https://www.edweek.org/teaching-learning/teachers-push-for-books-with-more-diversity-fewer-stereotypes/2019/06

The University of British Columbia. (2021, March 8). *Intersectionality: What is it and why it matters.* https://vpfo.ubc.ca/2021/03/intersectionality-what-is-it-and-why-it-matters/#:~:text=Intersectionality%20shows%20us%20that%20social,on%20and%20shapes%20the%20other

Additional Reading

Monroe, A. (2018). REAL talk, ALL voices, OUR truth: Moving the needle through transformational dialogue. *The Reformer* (pp. 71–76). Pakistan ASCD.

Schwartz, S. (2019, June 11). Teachers push for books with more diversity, fewer stereotypes. *EducationWeek.* https://www.edweek.org/teaching-learning/teachers-push-for-books-with-more-diversity-fewer-stereotypes/2019/06

Transformative Action for Diversity, Equity, Inclusion, and Belonging in Education

> We but mirror the world. ... If we could change ourselves, the tendencies in the world would also change. As a man changes his own nature, so does the attitude of the world change towards him. ... A wonderful thing it is and the source of our happiness. We need not wait to see what others do.
>
> —Mahatma Gandhi

Introduction

This chapter will provide a transformative roadmap for an authentic and inclusive environment by discussing intergroup relational and collaborative practices that focus on diversity, equity, inclusion, and belonging in educational settings.

Opening Reflection Questions

Directions: Before reading the chapter, take a few minutes to reflect on and respond to each of the questions below. These questions will help you become aware of your own perspectives, opinions, and experiences.

1. How do you become informed and aware of diverse cultures? Who or what influences your perceptions about cultures other than your own?
2. Identify and examine some wrong assumptions that have influenced your beliefs, attitudes, and actions.
3. Do you willfully connect with others from different cultures? How do you navigate cultural differences and welcome new experiences? How do you know that you have successfully affirmed and engaged with the diverse cultures that you experience?
4. Have you ever felt different or "othered" because of your cultural background? What are some ways "othering" behaviors were exhibited?
5. Do you hold yourself accountable for your continued learning and growth when it comes to awareness of those from diverse backgrounds? What are some personal checks and balances you employ to remain honest, vulnerable, and transparent in your perceptions of diverse sub-groups?

BRITTANI'S STORY*

Brittani, refreshed from summer break, opens the door to the cafeteria ready for the new school year. School starts next week. As per usual, there are two days set aside prior to the official start of school for professional development. Brittani, who is a veteran teacher, continues to hold on to hope that these two professional development days will provide her with new insight and instructional strategies that she can use to help her students grow academically and socially.

Upon entering the room, Brittani is greeted with by smiles, friendly affirmations, fist bumps, and high fives. She scans the room and notes all the new faces, and she hopes that at least most of her close colleagues have returned. Acknowledged by a table of her fellow veterans, Brittani heads in their direction. Navigating through tables and greeting other teachers and sharing light banter, she finally arrives at her final destination: "the table of honor" comprised of the veteran teachers who have weathered the storm for ten or more years.

The smiles and cheery glances last only a moment. As the principal clears his throat to begin his welcome address, a colleague signals to Brittani, pointing to an item on the agenda. The item reads, "Culturally Responsive Teaching." Sharing a quizzical look with her buddy, Ann, Brittani shrugs her shoulders and whispers, "What is that?" Ann replies, "I don't know. But I understand that it is something new and we are supposed to integrate cultural competencies as part of our lesson plans by the end of this marking period." She continues, "I don't even know what culturally responsive teaching is. I always try to use examples from various cultures as part of my lessons."

Brittani, who is popular among students and considered one of their favorite teachers, sees the blank stares of her colleagues at the table who overheard the whispers she shared with Ann. Brittani rolls her eyes and drops her head. She thinks to herself, "If they [her colleagues] would only build relationships with students, they would know their students' interests and be able to create diverse lessons so that students would feel seen and heard. This is where it starts. It starts with building healthy, nurturing relationships with students." The glimmer of hope that Brittani entered the cafeteria with has quickly waned. Now, she believes that "more of the same" will happen this school year.

Brittani values professional development as an effective way to update her instructional practices. Thus, her frustration is not about learning something new. Instead, Brittani is disgusted by the constant flow of "new" instructional approaches adopted by school leadership and mandated for implementation by the teachers. Over the last ten years, Brittani has been required to implement at least seven new instructional practices and programs introduced by school leaders. By the time she achieved a comfortable level of mastery with one approach, school leaders introduced another one that "had a proven track record of success." Although she is excited to learn more about culturally responsive teaching and understands that learning more about cultural competencies and best practices is long overdue, especially since student demographics are rapidly changing, she once again thinks, "More of the same ... I feel like a gerbil on a spinning wheel, constantly moving but going nowhere. All I want to do is 'show up' best for all of my students." This is a familiar metaphor for her, as Brittani is the high school biology teacher. She then slouches into a comfortable position in her chair and awaits the principal's message.

The vignette is based on a real-world experience of one of the authors.

This scenario might seem all too familiar to educators. It is common for a principal to introduce new instructional strategies to teachers, especially those strategies that promise an increase in student academic performance. Considering that the national benchmark for student achievement is determined by performance on high-stakes standardized tests, school district administrators and school leaders are motivated to constantly quantify their schools' snapshots of academic success and compare them with national averages. Systemic norms govern and regulate power and authority within groups in school settings. Accordingly, we find Brittani struggling to connect her personal commitment to her students and her value for improving her instructional practice with systemic norms that influence teacher agency within her current school environment.

There is a relationship between caring and power. Caring is the construct for a network of social relationships, the basis from which people realize freedom and genuine personhood (Noddings, 1992). Nonetheless, how one envisions "caring" depends on their unique worldview. Since we live in a world that we create with others, conversations addressing diverse worldviews should surface if a community where all comfortably coexist is the desired goal.

Creating Authentic Connections

Authentic connection is essential to building strong relationships between teachers and students and to providing students opportunities to learn about the cultural commonalities and differences between themselves and their peers (Hanser, 2023). On a deeper level, healthy teacher-student relationships help spark and sustain student engagement, support learning, and create meaningful student connections to learning content. Some teachers tend to be more authoritative with their students as opposed to being more humanistic, which can often create a void in their relationships with students (Fenner-McAdoo, 2021). Authentic connection affords all participants opportunities to learn from each other, eliminates cultural chasms, and enhances better communication within the classroom.

Statistics show that strong relationships between students and teachers have a significant impact on the well-being of students and on their ability to learn and stay engaged in school (Nguyen, 2021). More importantly, teacher-student relationships play a critical role in the cognitive development of students, which allows them to process new information, heal trauma, and value their learning (Bergman, 2023). Developing nurturing relationships with students requires teachers to have an awareness of their own biases and how these biases might impact their teaching practices and interactions with students (Hanser, 2023). Also, it is necessary for teachers to hone their relationship-building skills to fairly allow all students to share anecdotes and stories related to their cultures, traditions, family customs, and generational trends (Nguyen, 2021). Teachers must include resources in the classroom that are reflective of the cultural backgrounds of their students, along with activities that are reflective of the real world. Activities that promote authentic connection and collaboration can range from classroom discussions and project-based learning to meditation and mindfulness (The Learning Network, 2020).

The Ethics of Care and Empathy

The ethics of care and empathy imply connection. For Brittani, caring for her students is intimately connected to her own personal growth. Often described as a web or circle of relationships, the ethic of care is the development of interdependence rather than independence (Noddings, 1992). According to Beck (1992), living in relation to others is about achieving freedom by becoming "indissolubly linked" (p. 456) with those whose lives intersect with ours. Through a scientific exploration of humanness, Maturana and Varela (1987) point out that a basic feature of humanness is the relationships that we create with others. In other words, to be human is to engage in community.

Community and an ethic of caring arise from a web of relationships. As we co-create with others, the level of connection in the web is unequal. We care most for those with whom we have the most in common emotionally, physically, and culturally, because this is natural and comfortable (Sernak, 1998). In other words, we can relate to people like us with little to no effort. However, what happens to those relationships that extend beyond our intimate web or circle? Although students do not necessarily belong in the most intimate circle, the relationship to the teacher is, ideally, close (Noddings, 1992). Nonetheless, we must also consider real situations. Reflecting on current school communities, additional questions arise. Will teachers whose students are not of their own background, culture, and social systems be able to closely relate to them (Sernak, 1998)? Further, will teachers who espouse an ethic of caring comfortably coalesce in their own web, hoping that others who are more like these students take up the job? This dilemma brings us to our own personal consideration of enlarging our boundaries of empathy.

The notion of building community in schools raises issues that are often contradictory, such as individuality versus connection. How do we connect with others while maintaining our own identity? If it is community that we truly desire, then, like the ethic of care, relationships and responsibilities are its core and who we are anchors the bond.

Reflection is paramount to the ethics of care and empathy. Therefore, it is essential that we identify and validate personal values that are significant for us. The values that you identify reflect your past experiences and history. Accordingly, your values influence your attitudes, behaviors, and actions in a community.

Exploring Your Personal Values

Step 1: "What I Value Most Is ..."

From this list of values (both work and personal), select *five* that are most important to you, that are guides for how you behave, or that are components of what society considers a valuable way of life. Feel free to add any values of your own to this list.

achievement	family time	profitability
caring	flexibility	quality
caution	freedom	quantity
challenge	fun	respect
communication	growth	responsibility
competition	honesty & integrity	risk
creativity	human relationships	security
curiosity	individualism	service to others
customer focus	innovation	speed
determination	involvement	task-oriented
diversity	learning	teamwork
fairness	organization	uniqueness
cooperation	productivity	winning

Step 2: Elimination

Choose a partner. Each of you will take turns as "values presenter" and as coach. One by one, the coach asks the values presenter to eliminate one more value, until each person is left with only one.

Step 3: Articulation

Take a look at the top three values on your list. The coach asks the following questions.

   a. What do these values mean, exactly?
   b. What did you feel when I asked you to give up a core value?
   c. Have you ever felt this way before, at home or at work?
   d. How do you want to handle this situation if it arises in the future?

Connection in community involves compromise and negotiation. In this exercise the "values presenter" has strong emotions when asked to relinquish all but one personal value. Personal values are often ignored or disregarded in communities in which a dominant group prevails. In addition, emotions are either dismissed or misinterpreted, which results in an emotionally charged and divided community. Thus, communal respect and relationships begin to disintegrate from within and the basis of the caring relationship is compromised (Buber, 1988).

Communicative Action as a Solution

A common denominator in successful organizational systems is good communication. In the classroom, teacher-student relationships are paramount to the learning process. The communication medium between both participants must be authentic and it must be established by the teacher as a stratagem for creating an inclusive learning environment.

As stated in Chapter 3, communicative action is essential to maintaining relationships in the community. Social therapist Jürgen Habermas's theory of communicative action is defined as a process for achieving mutual understanding by coordinating the efforts of the participants through communication (Brookfield, 1988). Habermas explains that communicative action serves to transmit and renew cultural knowledge. Communicative action motivates the processing of cultural knowledge to create space for achieving mutual understanding (HRF, 2023). Mutual understanding is critical to the learning process because students from diverse backgrounds are often deprived of authentic reciprocity from teachers with different worldviews. Accordingly, cultural and social blind spots must shift from the peripheral to the primary focus of learning spaces.

Today's students are considerably different from those of previous generations. Therefore, teachers must have a better understanding of the cultural and social shifts of students. In order to actively engage all students, teachers must first examine the various aspects of effective communication. Statistics show that 60–90% of our communication with others is nonverbal, which clearly illustrates that body language is critically important (Economy, 2015). Teachers often fail to realize that students are keenly aware of their connection with them. In other words, students know if a teacher genuinely cares about them or not. A student's assessment of their connections with school leaders, teachers, and counselors is based on their interpretation of verbal and nonverbal exchanges with these individuals.

Successful teachers actively listen, demonstrate empathy, and provide and receive feedback from their students (Instagantt, 2023). They differentiate their communication styles to encourage a sense of belonging for all students. Strong teacher-student relationships become a norm that is evidenced in every aspect of the teaching and learning process. Teachers expect and require all students to think critically, take initiative, and furnish their feedback as part of the learning process because they can and want to. High-level engagement with students builds teachers' capacity to better understand the needs of all students. Student engagement as a teaching norm and practice assures that all learners have equitable access to learning, which best prepares students for academic and social success as well as college and/or career planning (Rudenstine et al., 2017).

Communicative Alignment

Communicative alignment refers to language and dialogic exchange between teachers and students. Communicative action that is comfortably aligned generates a better understanding between teachers and students. It provides the basis for teachers to create active learning strategies that encourage students to apply their cultural identities and knowledge to new situations. Likewise, it requires teachers to change the template of traditional lesson plans that primarily focus on grade-based standards and school district mandates to one that highlights differentiated instruction that meets students where they are academically, cognitively, culturally, emotionally, linguistically, physically, and behaviorally (Rudenstine et al., 2017). Additionally, studies show that communicative alignment has a positive impact on student learning, retention, and classroom equity, particularly for underrepresented students (Cornell Center for Teaching Innovation, 2023).

When teaching underrepresented students, it is imperative that teachers demonstrate their support by increasing their awareness and knowledge of students' cultural backgrounds. Lessons should motivate and engage students and afford them the opportunity to provide feedback (Cornell Center for Teaching Innovation, 2023). This will require teachers to develop their own cultural competence and create culturally immersed, inclusive classrooms that celebrate student differences (Samfrye, 2021). Culturally responsive teaching and lessons cultivate a learning space where all students feel welcomed and seen. Further, culturally responsive learning spaces are normed to dispel stereotypes, misconceptions, and false narratives that some teachers and students may have toward students from different cultures. The result is a safe space for authentic learning and communication.

Nonverbal and Verbal Communication

Non-verbal communication can often be more impactful than verbal communication. Particularly for students, nonverbal communication can influence their perception of the teacher. Gestures like body language, eye contact, and tone of voice are the three major components of nonverbal communication. The messages that are conveyed through these forms of expression are essential for creating a positive connection with students (Dardis Communications, 2023).

Listening is another communicative skill that is often overlooked when it comes to creating an inclusive learning environment. Active listening is not an innate skill that everyone possesses, but it can be learned. Research and communications specialist Gillian Parrish states that listening is "crucial to building a good classroom culture" (quoted in Steen, 2022). Parrish goes on to say that teachers need to emphasize the importance of listening to students and replicate it with their students (Steen, 2022). Teachers who lack active listening skills must learn to embrace silence, incorporate student responses into their lesson plans, look for ways to engage students who are introverts, pause before responding, and balance speaking and listening (Steen, 2023). Essentially, active listening is key to creating an inclusive learning environment that debunks myths about diverse cultures and instead empowers the voices of all students.

Effective verbal communication encompasses how humans deliver and receive messages. Verbal communication consists of two types of cues: direct and indirect. Direct verbal communication cues are clearly articulated statements of instructions, while indirect verbal cues are prompts that tend to be less obvious about what is expected and might come in the form of a question (White, 2021). More importantly, verbal and nonverbal communication cues are primarily derived from the cultural and social background of the teacher. The Sapir-Whorf hypothesis, also known as the *linguistic relativity hypothesis*, refers to the proposal that the particular language one speaks influences the way one thinks about reality (Lucy, 2001). Direct communication is usually considered to be characteristic of Western cultures, which tend to be individualistic, egalitarian, and analytical. Indirect communication is typical for Eastern cultures, which tend to be collective and hierarchical (Multicultural You, 2020). When nonverbal cues align with verbal communication it can increase trust, clarity, and rapport (Wertheim, 2022).

Micro- and Macroaggression

Microaggressions are brief and commonplace verbal, behavioral, and environmental indignities, whether intentional or unintentional, that communicate hostile, derogatory, or negative messages to individuals based on their marginalized group association (Solorzano et al., n.d.). Since the time of the original thirteen colonies that became the foundation of the United States, micro- and macroaggressions have been used to control, disrespect, and dehumanize underrepresented groups (Solorzano et al., n.d.). These messages can have a lasting psychological impact on underrepresented students in the classroom, where some teachers may process their opinions and perceptions through their personal biases and lifeworlds. Accordingly, educators must be conscious not to use communication to weaponize diversity. Instead, healthy communicative action should be leveraged to promote cultural competence.

Names, jargon, phrases, and gestures that were previously acceptable may now be defined as offensive. For example, after 86 years, the NFL team from Washington, DC, changed its name from the Redskins, which is considered offensive to Indigenous Americans, to the Commanders in 2020. In addition, after 121 years the MLB team from Cleveland changed its name and logo in 2021 from the Indians to the Guardians, because the use of an Indian as a mascot was deemed offensive to Indigenous Americans. A number of colleges have also changed their names, mascots, and/or logos for the same purpose. After 130 years of depicting a character of a Black woman stemming from slavery, PepsiCo changed the name and logo trademarks of their pancake and syrup products from Aunt Jemima to the Pearl Milling Company. The Aunt Jemima character was derived from a minstrel show in which the performers wore blackface, aprons, and bandanas (Alcorn, 2021). Despite backlash from civil rights groups beginning in the sixties and seventies, the company only changed the image of the Black woman wearing a bandana and slave-like clothing to a Black woman wearing a lace collar blouse and earrings in the eighties. The name and imagery change happened after protests intensified in response to the death of George Floyd. Top PepsiCo officials recognized that previous efforts to make Aunt Jemima a less racially denigrating image were not enough (Rosenberg, 2020). Although derogatory and offensive terminology can evolve, the root of its conception is a social sin that is a remnant of colonization and slavery. Consequently, educators must be aware of and adept in the underlying mandates for respectful communicative action with students and families from diverse cultures and backgrounds.

A macroaggression is a systemic institutional form of racism that is manifested in the philosophy, programs, policies, practices, and structures of governmental agencies, legal and judicial systems, health care organizations, educational institutions, and business and industry (Overbeeke, 2022). It is embedded in a number of organizations for the purpose of control and exclusion, and at times it is used to inflict harm against specific racial and ethnic groups (Overbeeke, 2022). When examining the current structure of public education in the United States, it is apparent that derivative forms of macroaggression exist in all levels of PK–12 education, particularly within the curricula. Curricula continue to reverberate sentiments of exclusivity and control. Textbooks, teaching resources, classroom decor, and other educational tools generally lack diversity, which can have a deep-seated effect on underrepresented students. Specifically, using textbooks and classroom resources published by predominantly White publishing companies is the status quo in American classrooms. As a result, curricula are not reflective of underrepresented students. A lack of identity connection with teachers and curricula hampers the intellectual and social growth of underrepresented students.

Communicative action is central to nurturing reciprocal relationships in a community. More specifically, teachers must participate in healthy communicative action with students to achieve shared meaning through nonstrategic processes. In particular, human social systems (educational settings) require that dialogue occurs. This dialogue, which is the outcome of the social interactions within the community, is central to the operation of the human social system (Maturana & Varela, 1987).

What Did We Learn in This Chapter?
A List of Key Takeaways

✓ The ethic of care is rooted in empathy. Empathy is the cause of care and concern for others. Care ethics emphasizes the need to commit to critical dialogue and thinking in order to view circumstances from multiple perspectives.

✓ A nurturing culture exists where there is understanding and respect for all members of a community. Dismantling institutionalized barriers that prohibit true inclusion will stimulate and enrich an educational experience that leads to increased innovation, collaboration, and global growth.

✓ The desire to communicate skillfully with others evolves from one's own confidence with their personal truth and esteem in the community in which they exist. To see, feel, and hear equity and social justice we must have the courage to acknowledge others and the way they interpret the world and be willing to work together in new ways.

Closing Reflection Exercise

Each of us have personal values that are influenced by our experiences. The data that we observe and keep from these experiences nurtures our beliefs. These beliefs are our personal histories and "backstories" that we naturally carry into any social system.

Step 1:

What are examples of human social systems (communities) to which you belong (e.g., family, church, school, organizations, etc.)? List the top three.

Choose one of the human social systems from your list. Describe ways in which members of your community are connected.

Step 2:
Keeping in mind the community that you previously identified, what are some of its embedded values? (Embedded values are aspects of goodwill, principles, or standards of behavior integrated into an established system or organization.)

Step 3:
Name two existing norms that are associated with these embedded values. (An existing norm is a designated standard of performance, or a rule that is enforced by members of a community.)

An example:
Step 1:
    a. Human social systems to which I belong: Family, School, Gym
    b. School community connections: Want to teach, want the best for children; desire to make a difference

Step 2:
    a. School community embedded values: Progressive student performance, academic rigor, high-quality instruction, student engagement, student persistence

Step 3:
    a. School community norms: Instruction is purposeful and relevant. School culture motivates a sense of belonging. Students will be good citizens.

Unpacking the activity:
The intent of this activity is for you to self-reflect on your personal values and how they relate to the values of the social groups you belong to. As you examine your personal values and beliefs, start to make connections to your current workplace. Note the connections *and* disconnects that you identified.

    Recognize that your lifeworld frames the context for your understanding of what you experience. Understanding that we innately use information from our personal experiences to make sense of our current reality validates who we are within our community. Who we are within our community furnishes resources for communicative action.

References

Alcorn, C. (2021, February 9). Aunt Jemima finally has a new name. *CNN*. https://www.cnn.com/2021/02/09/business/aunt-jemima-new-name/index.html

Beck, U. (1992). *Risk society: Towards a new modernity.* Sage Publications.

Bergman, R. (2023, March 9). *How to create authentic learning experiences to engage students.* Flocabulary Inc. https://blog.flocabulary.com/authentic-learning-to-engage-students/

Brookfield, S. (1988). What is communicative action? In "Democratizing classroom discussion," *Handbook of research on ethical challenges in higher education leadership and administration.* IGI Global.

Buber, M. (1988). *The knowledge of man: Selected essays.* Humanity Books.

Cornell Center for Teaching Innovation. (2023). Teaching strategies. teaching.cornell.edu. https://teaching.cornell.edu/teaching-resources/teaching-cornell-guide/teaching-strategies

Dardis Communications. (2023). *3 key elements of nonverbal communication.* https://www.dardiscommunications.com/2018/08/3-key-elements-of-nonverbal-communication/

Economy, P. (2015). *18 ways to send the right message with body language.* Inc.com. https://www.inc.com/peter-economy/18-ways-to-make-your-body-talk-the-language-of-success.html

Fenner-McAdoo, E. (2021, May 14). *Exploring classroom management styles.* teachhub.com. https://www.teachhub.com/classroom-management/2021/05/exploring-classroom-management-styles/

Hanser, C. (2023). *Building deeper connections in the classroom.* Linc: The Learning Innovation Catalyst. https://blog.linclearning.com/building-deeper-connections-in-the-classroom

Health Research Funding (HRF). (2023). *Habermas theory of communicative action explained*. Definitions and examples of theory. https://healthresearchfunding.org/habermas-theory-communicative-action-explained/

Instagantt. (2023). *A guide on top 10 skills for effective communication*. Instagantt.com. https://instagantt.com/project-management/top-10-skills-for-effective-communication?_kx=8dYYA9H-zkXk KG8MX9MOj3UC04IT8zqKAKqeYC6wYyQ%3D.TbhCjk

The Learning Network. (2020, August 27). 7 activities to build community and positive classroom culture during online learning. *New York Times*. https://www.nytimes.com/2020/08/27/learning/7-activities-to-build-community-and-positive-classroom-culture-during-online-learning.html#link-2cb097e0

Lucy, J. A. (2001). Sapir-Whorf hypothesis. In *International encyclopedia of the social & behavioral sciences*. Science Direct. https://www.sciencedirect.com/topics/psychology/sapir-whorf-hypothesis

Maturana, H. R., & Varela, F. J. (1987). *The tree of knowledge: The biological roots of human understanding*. New Science Library, Shambala Publications.

Multicultural You. (2020, June 22). *Direct and indirect communication styles*. https://multiculturalyou.com/2020/06/22/direct-and-indirect-communication-styles/

Nguyen, H. (2021). The "how" of building deeper relationships with students. *Edutopia*. https://www.edutopia.org/article/how-building-deeper-relationships-students

Noddings, N. (1992). *The challenge to care in schools: An alternative approach to education*. Teachers College Press.

Overbeeke, T. (2022). *Everyday indignities: Microaggressions, microassaults, microinsults, microinvalidation, microinequities, and macroaggressions*. Society for Academic Emergency Medicine. https://www.saem.org/about-saem/academies/adiemnew/education/dei-curriculum/microaggressions-macroaggressions-microinequity-microinsults

Rosenberg, L. (2020, June 17). *Here's why Quaker is finally changing Aunt Jemima's highly problematic logo*. distractify.com. https://www.distractify.com/p/aunt-jemima-logo-evolution

Rudenstine, A., Schaef, S., & Bacallo, D. (2017, June 15). *What does it mean to meet students where they are?* Competencyworks Blog. Aurora Institute. https://aurora-institute.org/cw_post/what-does-it-mean-to-meet-students-where-they-are/

Samfrye. (2021, August 3). *6 ways teachers can better support Black students in the classroom.* boredteachers.com. https://www.boredteachers.com/post/6-ways-teachers-can-better-support-black-students-in-the-classroom

Sernak, K. (1998). *School leadership: Balancing power with caring.* Teachers College Press.

Solorzano, D., Ceja, M., & Yosso, T. (n.d.). *Resource guide: Avoiding microaggressions in the classroom.* Reinert Center for Transformative Teaching and Learning. Saint Louis University. https://www.slu.edu/cttl/resources/resource-guides/microaggressions.pdf

Steen, M. (2022). *When teachers become better listeners, students become better learners—Here's why.* Resilient Educator. https://resilienteducator.com/classroom-resources/teachers-listening-skills/#:~:text=Being%20listened%20to%20deepens%20student%20learning&text=%E2%80%9CThe%20effect%20of%20a%20good,sincerely%2C%20then%20they%20blossom.%E2%80%9D

Steen, M. (2023). *5 ways teachers can boost their listening skills.* Resilient Educator. https://resilienteducator.com/classroom-resources/teachers-boost-listening-skills/

Wertheim, E. (2022). *The importance of effective communication.* Helpguide.org. https://www.helpguide.org/articles/relationships-communication/nonverbal-communication.htm

White, D. (2021). *Verbal cues in communication: Definition & examples.* Study.com. https://study.com/academy/lesson/verbal-cues-in-communication-definition-examples.html

CHAPTER 6

Creating Safe Space for Multicultural Excellence

Life is to be lived, not controlled, and humanity is won by continuing to play in face of certain defeat.

—Ralph Ellison

Introduction

Creating space for multicultural excellence requires a responsive approach to inclusion for people from diverse cultures. This chapter will provide approaches to identifying and decoding White privilege and entitlement as well as the power dynamics of dominance, and it will offer practical ways to eradicate these barriers to create healthy learning spaces that morally, ethically, and authentically amplify all voices in order to establish co-created, actively engaged, egalitarian school communities and campuses.

Opening Reflection Exercise

1. Think about all the individuals you interact with and are connected to in some way (i.e., the "others" in Figure 4.1). Select an individual or sub-group you are most familiar with, then identify an individual or

sub-group that you infrequently connect with which evokes deep personal feelings of uneasiness or discomfort.

2. Candidly and critically engage in self-reflection. Imagine that a person from each of the groups you selected is asking you the questions below. Journal your responses and note your emotional reactions.

Self-Reflection Cues:

- Do you know me?
- What do you know about me?
- Do you care about me?
- Do you want to know more about me?
- What are your assumptions?
- How can we better understand each other?
- Do I matter to you?

3. Review your reflection notes. What do you see, hear, and feel? Have you gained any new insights?
4. How do you authentically engage *all* students in order to strengthen and sustain your awareness and acceptance of diversity and multiculturalism?

MR. CURCIO'S STORY, PART 2: THE INTRODUCTION OF MRS. DAWN*

Mr. Curcio, in his endeavor to reexamine the status quo at Saintville High School (SHS), acknowledged that he must start the process with self-reflection. He started by unpacking his personal vision for SHS. The following questions prompted his reflection.

Self-Reflection Exercise
Personal Vision Check-In:

- What would I like to see my school become, for its own sake?
- Who should my school serve?

- What kind of students/learners will it have?
- What type of learning services and support should it offer?
- If I had this sort of organization, what would it bring *me*? How would it allow my *personal vision* to flourish?

Although Mr. Curcio's thoughts focused on the entire SHS community, he noticed that his attention was drawn to the new enrollments. He vividly recollected what community members were saying, and the changed disposition of the teachers in particular. What did "Our town is beginning to look like Liberty (a richly diverse neighboring community)" really mean?

While Mr. Curcio envisioned an SHS that would truly welcome and embrace all students and families, he recalled his initial response when he learned about the new students who were going to enroll in his school. His expectations were high because he anticipated that families from the luxury housing would yield "good" students like those already attending Saintville. What he failed to factor into his personal equation were "those students" from the subsidized housing. The realization set in when he saw the parents who began to trickle in with their children to complete the student enrollment package.

"Those people," "ghetto," "ignorant," "illiterate," "rough," "unruly," "poor," and harsher words made him cringe as he recalled his own first impressions. These initial stereotypes flooded his thoughts. Aghast and bewildered by his own perceptions, he got up and took a walk. The bell just rang and it was the passing period.

As he walked the halls, he heard laughter and the slap of high fives, of which he himself received a few. He saw the smiles on the faces of his students. Most of the teachers were standing at their classroom doors welcoming students with jovial banter, a special handshake, or a brief motivational call and response. What struck him was the burgeoning friendship between Rashawn Frazier (an African American student) and Brandon Land (a White student). Brandon's family was well-respected in Saintville. His father owned the most popular restaurant in town. It was also heart-warming to see Courtney DeLuca (an Italian American student) giggling with Saanvi Patel (a South Asian student) as she helped her get her books from her locker. Courtney's mother worked in the mayor's office and her father was a partner at a reputable law firm. As he returned to his office, he questioned himself, his perceptions, his beliefs, and his reality. From that brief walk, he learned a lesson from his students. And he was determined to make this new normal at Saintville High School flourish and thrive.

Mrs. Dawn is the first Black assistant principal (AP) at Saintville High School. She, like Mr. Curcio, is Saintville born-and-raised. She's been the AP at SHS for seven years. She applied for the position of principal and assumed that she was a shoo-in for the job, since she was the interim principal for a year and a half, filling in for the veteran principal, who had taken ill in the middle of the school year. However, Mr. Curcio was selected to fill the position.

Mrs. Dawn completed her teaching fieldwork and practicum work in Liberty. She started her teaching career in Saintville and then accepted a position as an instructional coach in Liberty when the opportunity became available. She spent a number of years in Liberty, and her work organizing and leading the data team as well as developing professional learning communities was credited for the positive uptick in standardized test scores across all student sub-groups. In particular, Mrs. Dawn achieved notable success with underrepresented students.

Mrs. Dawn, who regularly checks her calendar, noticed a new meeting placed on her schedule. Mr. Curcio, whom she meets with officially twice per week but chats with all the time throughout the day, scheduled a meeting and flagged it as "urgent" on her schedule. She also noticed that the meeting duration was one and a half hours. The participants included the entire administrative team, instructional coaches, the special education department chair, school counselors, and the high school caseworker. It was rare for Mr. Curcio to meet with school leaders during the day for such a long period of time. She wondered what was going on.

The meeting began. Frank (Mr. Curcio), who is characteristically warm and confident, seemed unusually agitated and on edge. As she waited for the agenda to be circulated, Mrs. Dawn noticed her colleagues also showed signs of discomfort in the awkward silence. As per usual, Frank opened the meeting with a welcome and brief update. As part of his message, he mentioned that there would be no agenda. What he wanted was for the team to bring their full, authentic selves into the space. He continued to respectfully enforce the norms of safety, trust, and a no judgment zone.

Frank started the meeting with an icebreaker. Through revisiting his own personal vision, he was forced to identify and examine his personal values and norms as they related to his practice and how they impacted his leadership style. Needless to say, the outcomes from this activity startled him and rocked him to his core. Frank was hoping that the school leadership team would have a similar experience. He thought, "We MUST be honest with ourselves first and be willing to unpack our 'stuff' in order for us to 'show up' 100% for each other, and for the teachers, students, and families that we serve." He further noted, "our students seem to get it, so we need to get it too."

The vignette is based on a real-world experience of one of the authors.

Cultural and Social Capital: The Collective Benefit

With systems that are imposed rather than established from within, individual capacity to develop critical consciousness is stagnated. America's colonial experience has given marginalized groups little opportunity to fully engage as cultural actors because culture has been defined by the dominant elite, who do not share the same reality (Freire, 1987). As we endeavor to reimagine educational spaces and learning communities, where the needs of all students are met and multicultural excellence is emboldened, perceptions of the status quo must be deeply examined.

Variations in student academic success are attributed to several factors. Cultural norms and values, the academic and disciplinary climate of the school, teacher-student relationships, student social networks, parent expectations and obligations to educating their children, and parent-school relationships all have great value. Creating a nurturing support system that encourages student success and provides all students with equitable access to resources helps students flourish throughout their academic journey and beyond.

Humans act according to their self-awareness (Akbar, 1996). Akbar explains that as humans, we act as we have been taught. In other words, we are products of manipulated beliefs. As such, we teeter between perceptions of illusion versus reality. Nonetheless, concentrating on negative beliefs will impede the advancement of any desire to value the true identities of all. We must value all of humanity as cultural actors that are defined by who they are and not by their names, what they look like, or where they are from.

Strong academic preparation and the development of soft skills provide a solid foundation for a promising life trajectory. In other words, students with high academic and social capital are apt to be high achievers and socially capable. On the other hand, students with low social capital are lower achievers and socially debilitated (Howard, 2003). Minority and low-SES students are less likely to be academically prepared for college and life beyond high school because of environmental and social impediments (Howard, 2003). Unequal school, family, and neighborhood resources as well as the lack of peer support are major barriers for these students.

Mindfully establishing a culture of equity and hope in learning spaces is the transformative approach needed to move school communities from a segregationist construct toward educating each and every student to high academic and social standards. Unapologetically calling out and then collectively identifying and dismantling the root causes of America's polarized education system ushers in restorative healing and ignites hope for a decolonized system that is fair and just for all members of the social system.

Defining Multicultural Education

Multicultural education is defined as a process that recognizes the disadvantages of students, regardless of socioeconomic status, race, disability, or zip code. The educational strategies include supportive initiatives designed to ensure that all students attain the same kind of education. As a direct result of multicultural education, educational accommodations, student interventions, and wraparound services are accessible to ensure that all students thrive.

Multicultural education in the classroom provides a vision of success along with a medium of hope for the voiceless. Research shows that when students learn more about their history and culture, they generally excel more in the classroom and are less likely to end up experiencing adverse events such as imprisonment or unemployment (NCES, 2022). Studies have also shown that students become more involved in class and their grades improve when curricula are diverse (NCES, 2022). More importantly, multicultural education reintroduces relevancy into education, which plays a significant role in how students think, feel, live, and envision themselves in society.

One factor that was disturbingly disregarded during busing and the integration of White schools was the animus mindset of White teachers. Most White teachers had little to no association with or empathy for Black people. Despite the impact of this major sociopolitical change in education, school districts and government organizations failed to implement adequate sensitivity training to grow awareness and build the capacity of school administrators, teachers, and other school officials to prepare them for this drastic social change. Instead, White educators were forced to accept students of color in their classroom. Students were not welcomed, and educators remained entrenched in their personal biases and cultural deficits. Today, some of those same conditions are still prevalent in U.S. school districts and, more importantly, in classrooms.

The racial imbalance in the educational system fosters cultural illiteracy through the lack of diversity in curricula and the failure to train current and prospective teachers on the rudiments of multicultural education. Many public school districts are ill-equipped to adequately educate students from diverse groups. Specifically, schools continue to implement curricula through a dominant culture lens that remains exclusionary of its marginalized populations. In a country that is noted to have some of the best colleges and universities, as well as inventors, scientists, and highly skilled persons in various professions, developing innovative programs and guidelines to re-create an educational system reflective of all students is a reasonable expectation.

A major part of continued learning comes from inside the classroom, through daily interactions with students. This includes understanding students' psychological, social, and emotional health as well as their aspirations. In doing so, multicultural education provides a basis for creating lesson plans that are creative, engaging, and diverse. Also, classroom design should convey a welcoming environment that reflects the social and cultural makeup of students. Studies show that students from diverse backgrounds often excel in class when their teachers employ this format in the classroom (NCES, 2022). This process should not be interpreted as an educational project in which students are the subjects of an experiment. It is simply an effective approach to developing teaching strategies and techniques for increasing academic achievement in the classroom that involves social, emotional, and inclusive learning. In the same manner as the teachers, book publishers need to change their content to be reflective of all students.

Monocultural Dominance Versus Multiculturalism

Public education today continues to have a stronghold on the shaping of students from preschool and kindergarten to post-secondary education. Its impact is tragically inadequate, particularly for Black, Brown, and Indigenous American students. These students remain victims of a monolithic system that still touts Eurocentric ideologies. Dr. Carter G. Woodson states in his book *The Mis-Education of the Negro*, "Blacks of his day were being culturally indoctrinated, rather than taught in American schools. This condition causes Blacks to become dependent and to seek out inferior places in the greater society ... which they are a part of" (Woodson, 1933). The voices of historically marginalized sub-groups are still silenced in the education system. Both implicit and explicit Eurocentrism serve as the glue that continue to hold monolithic curricula in place. Multiculturalism acknowledges the student mosaic. Success with multicultural education can only be achieved when educators are collectively impartial as they enact the teaching and learning process.

MEET MR. BRANCH*

Crestview College (CC) has an Educational Opportunity Fund (EOF) staff of four counselors and one director. During the Pre-College Summer Institute, the Director of EOF requires that each counselor manage a specific component of the program. The components are academic, counseling, leadership, and residential. In addition to this assignment, each counselor is assigned a small group of incoming freshmen to supervise and support.

During the past summer's program, Mr. Branch, a twenty-three-year veteran EOF counselor, was responsible for the academic component of the summer institute. He scheduled student classes and ensured that all students completed their placement tests. Mr. Branch was also assigned a small group of incoming freshmen to monitor and mentor.

As part of the daily schedule for CC's Pre-College Summer Institute, students are in their small groups from 1:30 to 3:00 p.m. EOF counselors use this time to engage in team-building activities, coach students on skills development, and meet with them individually to develop academic goals and review their academic progress. Each counselor is responsible for leading their small group. However, Mr. Branch refused to facilitate his small group sessions. Instead, he assigned a graduate assistant to conduct the sessions on his behalf. Regardless of the program's norms and the oversight he provided for small groups in past years, Mr. Branch believed that this time he should be solely responsible for the summer program's academic component.

When Mr. Branch was confronted by the EOF director and asked to lead his group as per the program's standard of operations, he stated, "These students today are so disrespectful. I don't get it. I'm trying to help them, and they won't listen to what I'm telling them to do. They need to understand that what I say goes!" He then threatened to file a grievance with the union if he was forced to deal with "these students." Needless to say, the graduate assistant continued to facilitate the small group for the remainder of the summer institute.

Although Mr. Branch was an EOF counselor at CC for twenty-three years, he devoted the past ten years primarily to his work with the union. Mr. Branch's fellow EOF counselors feel that the needs of his students are being ignored because he is more concerned about his union activities than fulfilling his duties as a counselor. In addition, the counselors have noticed that Mr. Branch's apathy and lack of commitment are impacting the relationships that they have with their own groups of students. In particular, they are disturbed by what they are hearing from their students during their meetings. "I don't understand why I have to come to my meeting when others don't have to." "I'm trying, but why are you so hard on me? Some students don't even have to meet with their counselor." "I'm really busy, so why do we need to meet so much? I'm coming to my appointments, but there are other students who don't have to meet with their counselor and it's okay."

During the academic year, the EOF counselors maintain a full schedule, which includes seeing an average of six students per day. Mr. Branch only accepts three student appointments per day. The EOF director, after reviewing student performance data, is seeing the impact of Mr. Branch's apathy and disconnection with the EOF program. The academic component (which Mr. Branch oversees) has been mediocre, which is evidenced by the drastic dip in student performance outcomes. In particular, Mr. Branch's students

are failing courses and are not attending any of the program's mandatory workshops and events. With a heavy sigh,
the EOF director mumbles to herself, "The students are not
thriving. Something must change! And this is a battle that
I will not lose."

*The vignette is based on a real-world experience of one of
the authors.*

Creating Safe Space for Liberated Voices

Educators who are authentically connected to their students will
be able to recognize traumatized students by changes in their
behavior and class participation, and therefore be able to address
barriers resulting from the impact of traumatic experiences. In the
vignette we meet Mr. Branch, who is an EOF counselor. The EOF
Program provides services for students who need academic, socio-
emotional, and financial support. In particular, underrepresented
students identify programs like EOF as safe spaces where they feel
valued and will receive high-quality academic and socio-emotional
support as well as access to wraparound services. EOF counselors are entrusted to lead, coach, counsel, and mentor students
from educationally and economically disadvantaged backgrounds.
Accordingly, the EOF students depended on Mr. Branch to support
and advocate for them.

Morality in an ethic of caring is contextual. What "ought" to be
is a norm, which reflects the moral consciousness of a community
(Habermas, 1991). Critical consciousness evolves as the community
develops and situations arise. The ethic of care requires devotion
and loyalty (Noddings, 1992). This commitment involves a connected
knowing, awareness, and acceptance of others. Although the caring
relationship may change over time, the bond remains, and what
the participants will to be the norm is binding on everyone within
the community.

The Impact of Trauma

Historically marginalized students walk around with inherited antagonisms and are plagued by micro- and macroaggressions intended to oppress them. Bullying and discriminatory beliefs and behaviors, which are commonly referred to as "isms," are major causes of trauma. These destructive beliefs and behaviors are commonplace within educational settings. Accordingly, incidents of oppression and discrimination aggravate trauma and trigger symptoms of stress and anxiety, panic attacks, and many other mental, emotional, and/or physical health conditions.

Trauma has the capacity to overwhelm our ability to cope. For example, students who experience homelessness and hunger are victims of daily trauma. Recognizing the traumatic effects of hunger, the Black Panther Party implemented a breakfast program in 1969 that fed thousands of hungry children nationwide. As a result, school officials noticed a positive change in students: they were more alert and engaged in class. In 1975, the U.S. government replicated the program by creating the School Breakfast Program, which continues to this day. While traumatic experiences are increasingly prevalent among students, most recently, researchers have noted that the COVID-19 pandemic has disproportionately affected African American, Latinx, and Indigenous American families (Hoover, 2021).

Trauma has a devastating impact on a student's ability to learn, and a trauma-informed pedagogical approach is grounded first and foremost in an awareness of the signs of trauma among one's students. These signs include difficulty focusing, retaining, and recalling information; anger, helplessness, or dissociation when stressed; and anxiety about exams, public speaking, and assignments. It can also affect students' functional IQ (Perry & Winfrey, 2021).

Trauma-informed practice requires teachers to create classroom communities that promote student well-being and learning (Marquart et al., 2020). In addition, developing trusting and nurturing teacher-student relationships is central to the development of a positive, caring, safe, and welcoming learning environment. Of equal importance, professional development and training helps teachers to become trauma-informed and adept at recognizing the pervasiveness of trauma in the world, so that they can effectively respond to students affected by trauma (King, 2021).

Mattering is a belief that we are significant to the world around us (Mercurio, 2022). Social psychologists note that mattering arises from two primary experiences: feeling valued and adding value to those around us. In the context of education, mattering and well-being are inseparable. Mattering generates self-efficacy and enables every member of the learning community to thrive. Conveying to students that they matter and acting accordingly is a highly effective response that mitigates micro- and macroaggressions and trauma.

> The mediocre teacher tells.
> The good teacher explains.
> The superior teacher demonstrates.
> The great teacher inspires.
>
> —William Arthur Ward

Culturally Responsive Teaching

For decades, Black and other marginalized students have demanded culturally responsive education. Culturally responsive teaching acknowledges students' stories and cultural and social perspectives. It is a research-based approach that embeds meaningful connections between what students learn in schools and their culture, language, and life experiences. Specifically, culturally responsive instruction is teaching in a way that students can understand. By acknowledging students' prior knowledge and exploring their interests and extracurricular activities, teachers incorporate relatable experiences into their lessons.

As change agents, teachers must recognize and address the inequities that exist in education. Classroom activities must be intellectually challenging and culturally relevant for students, from the books they read, to the videos they watch, to the tests they take

(Mohammed, 2023). When teaching a particular subject, teachers should connect students to the content. For instance, a teacher in Louisiana employed her creativity by using Beyoncé's song "Formation" to teach her class geometry (Wilkins, 2016). Also, many teachers employ mindfulness activities in the classroom to help students relax their minds, relieve stress in their bodies, and improve concentration (Cole, 2021).

Example: When teaching math, the teacher can explain how mathematics plays a major role in our everyday life, from calculating the stock market and playing professional sports to devising a flight plan for the NASA space program. The teacher can incorporate project-based learning techniques that refer to brilliant trailblazers like Katherine Johnson, Dorothy Vaughan, Mary Jackson, or Mae Jamison. Pictures of heroes and heroines of color should be displayed in the classroom throughout the year. When teaching math and science in the classroom, teachers should refer to notable individuals who have been successful in STEM fields along with conveying to students how these role models' successes apply to students' everyday lives.

Example: Math or science teachers can enhance creativity in their students by incorporating science-based projects illustrating examples of Ralph Victor Gilles's design of the Chrysler 300, or Lonnie Johnson's creation of the Super Soaker water gun, or Patricia Era Bath's use of science and math to create a method for combining laser and ultrasound to remove cataracts.

The change initiative of cultural responsiveness provides a pragmatic means for facilitating ethical change related to the shifting of values, assumptions, and beliefs affecting judgment. Critical dialogue relative to structure, power through voice, relationship connectivity, and individual and organization generativity are essential elements of culturally responsive teaching practice.

Within today's schools, educators have the capacity to transform the educational system from culturally suppressive to inclusive and equitable. They are powerful agents of change that have the capacity to collaboratively demand transformative change in learning spaces. Within their own sphere of influence, they can voice, model, and demonstrate their shared meaning for inclusive education, which will provide a high-quality education and social experience for all students and families, and for each other.

Weaving a Warm Blanket

> Think of various perspectives as threads in a blanket. Even if each thread is of high quality, we only get warmth as the strands are woven together well. The more threads intertwine, the more warmth the blanket will capture. At some point before the entire blanket is woven, a tipping point is reached. That is when a true sense of community is achieved.
>
> —Alicia S. Monroe

Education as a Practice of Freedom

"All men are created equal" and "to the republic for which it stands, one nation, under God, indivisible, with liberty and justice for all" are two of many patriotic tenets that frame our national creed. The American system of democracy suggests that the "ultimate political authority is vested in the people" (Cronin, 1987, p. 304). However, oppressive attitudes and beliefs are entrenched in America's social stratification system. Standing on the shoulders of ancestors, whose unrelenting will to survive defeated the vicious attempts of forced assimilation by European colonists, fuels the persistent, never-ending struggle of historically marginalized groups to transcend the Eurocentric boundaries of privilege in order to legitimize the egalitarian society that America professes itself to be.

Disposing of contentious colonial connotations that negate the lived experiences of the people purges them of the baggage that hinders their progress (Memmi, 1965). Freire's (1987) model of education involves the practice of liberty because it frees the educator and the student from silence. In providing the oppressed with educational strategies for emancipation, there is a forum for dialogue that values the perspectives of all people.

Liberation is a dynamic activity in which the educator and student are actively involved in dialogical education (Freire, 1987). The ideal speech situation and the rules of reason, coupled with a sense of solidarity, establish legitimacy and the necessary conditions for pluralism (Habermas, 1991), which rejects assimilation to one dominant culture and instead promotes a "mosaic." As America becomes more diverse, it is imperative that educators invest sufficient time to develop true dialogue in order to adequately serve the needs of all students. Once this level of critical consciousness is achieved, the dominant group will be better able to embrace difference and work to make changes that will benefit the American "mosaic," instead of continuing to bolster and reinforce the traditional status quo of the "melting pot."

What Did We Learn in This Chapter?
A List of Key Takeaways

- ✓ Self-reflection is the first step in a continuous healthy practice of acceptance, inclusion, and growth in cultural competence.
- ✓ Empathy energizes each of the dimensions of the authentically engaged community (Figure 4.1). Accordingly, an ethic of care provides the community with norms of safety, acceptance, respect, trust, forgiveness, and the empowerment of every voice that work collectively to establish and achieve a shared vision.
- ✓ Culturally responsive instruction elevates and dignifies cultural differences. It does not teach to a certain race or water down the established content.
- ✓ Harmonious coexistence results from transformative and equitable practices that dismantle injustices, White privilege, and entitlement. In a community in which all voices are honored and amplified, norms for a true American mosaic are espoused, established, and embedded.

Closing Reflection Questions

Directions: Consider what you have learned in this chapter as you respond to the questions below. Be aware of how new information and understandings can help you reframe your ideas and opinions.

- ✓ What communicative actions have you employed that have enabled you to successfully relate to students from diverse backgrounds?
- ✓ Active listening is an important practice for creating authentic relationships. On a scale of 1 to 10, with 10 being the highest, how do you rate yourself as an active listener? How has your active listening connected you to others in your community?
- ✓ In an examination of cultural deficits versus cultural competence, what are your perceptions of others in your community? What will you do to better appreciate and understand differences? How will you bridge the gaps in your cultural understanding?
- ✓ How will you hold yourself accountable for your continued growth and awareness of diverse cultures, narratives, and experiences? What will you do to educate others?

References

Akbar, N. (1996). Psychological legacy of slavery. In *Breaking the chains of psychological slavery* (pp. 1–26). Mind Productions and Associates. https://pdfcoffee.com/breaking-the-chains-of-psychological-slavery-pdf-free.html

Cole, L. (2021). 10 classroom mindfulness activities for students. *Mentalup.* https://www.waterford.org/resources/mindfulnes-activities-for-kids/

Cronin, T. (1987). Leadership and democracy. In J. T. Wren (Ed.), *The leader's companion* (pp. 303–309). The Free Press.

Freire, P. (1987). *Education for critical consciousness*. The Continuum Publishing Company.

Habermas, J. (1991). *Moral consciousness and communicative action*. MIT Press.

Hoover, E. (2021, August 3). Who's had Covid-19? A national survey of students reveals disparities. *Chronicle of Higher Education*. https://www.chronicle.com/article/whos-had-covid-19-a-national-survey-of-students-reveals-disparities

Howard, T. (2003). A tug of war for our minds: African American high school students' perceptions of their academic identities and college aspirations. *The High School Journal, 87*(1), 4–17.

King, K. (2021, November 26). What does it mean to be trauma-informed? *Psychology Today*. https://www.psychologytoday.com/us/blog/lifespan-perspectives/202111/what-does-it-mean-be-trauma-informed

Marquart, M., Báez, J., & Carello, J. (2020, October 9). *Essential trauma-informed teaching tools* [Webinar]. Trauma-Informed Teaching and Learning Blog. https://traumainformedteaching.blog/2020/10/29/essential-trauma-informed-online-teaching-tools/

Mercurio, Z. (2022, November 15). *How to create mattering at work*. Zach's Blog. https://www.zachmercurio.com/2022/11/mattering-at-work/

Memmi, A. (1965). *The colonizer and the colonized*. Beacon Press.

Mohammed, S. (2023, April 10). Black children deserve representation in STEM fields. *Afro News*. https://afro.com/black-children-deserve-representation-in-stem-fields/?utm_medium=email&utm_source=rasa_io&utm_campaign=newsletter

National Center for Education Statistics (NCES). (2022). *Back to school statistics*. Institute of Education Sciences. U.S. Department of Education. https://nces.ed.gov/fastfacts/display.asp?id=372

Noddings, N. (1992). *The challenge to care in schools: An alternative approach to education*. Teachers College Press.

Perry, B., & Winfrey, O. (2021). *What happened to you?: Conversations on Trauma, resilience, and healing*. Flatiron Books.

Wilkins, V. (2016, March 15). New Orleans teacher remixes Beyonce song to teach math lesson. *ABC News*. https://abcnews.go.com/

Lifestyle/orleans-teacher-remixes-beyonce-song-teach-math-lesson/story?id=37657602

Woodson, C. G. (1933). *The mis-education of the Negro*. The Associated Publishers.

Additional Reading

American University School of Education. (2021). *How to incorporate mindfulness in the classroom*. https://soeonline.american.edu/blog/mindfulness-in-the-classroom/

Blakemore, E. (2021). *How the Black Panthers' breakfast program both inspired and threatened the government*. history.com. https://www.history.com/news/free-school-breakfast-black-panther-party

Monroe, A. (2006). *Co-creation: Shifting the source of policy-making power* [Unpublished doctoral dissertation]. Rowan University.

Author Biographies

Alicia S. Monroe, EdD, is a PK–20 experienced educator and international education consultant. She has served as classroom teacher, supervisor, assistant principal, principal, assistant superintendent, adjunct professor, education consultant, and career coach. Her research on co-creative dialogue in culturally proficient schools, provides a glimpse into the sociodynamics  of school communities and methods of self-correction that support student achievement. Her notable success in creating a culture of belonging and achievement in schools along with her expertise in developing equity and access models that frame educational opportunities for all students are the core of the ongoing professional learning and support she provides to school districts. A sought-after speaker and facilitator, Monroe has presented her research at several national and international conferences.

At Rowan University, Monroe has taught undergraduate, graduate, and doctoral courses in diversity and inclusion. As an adjunct faculty member in the Africana Studies program, she teaches a course that she designed titled "Black Lives Matter: An Ethnographic Perspective of the Movement." She is currently responsible for three research studies focused on first-year initiative, neurodiversity, and effective student engagement with career services. Her partnership with the Office of Accessibility Services, Autism PATH program, and the Center for Neurodiversity has yielded impactful collaborative planning, student mentoring and coaching, and the creation of employer pathways and pipelines designed to provide diversability students and alumni with opportunities to secure and sustain meaningful internships and gainful employment.

Dr. Monroe is also the CEO and founder of Solutions for Sustained Success, LLC, which provides professional learning and other services in the areas of education, leadership, organizational change, change management, diversity and inclusion, and equity and access. Through her private practice, Dr. Monroe serves as national faculty for the Association for Supervision and Curriculum Development (ASCD). The whole child/whole student/whole educator framework that she was instrumental in designing and developing is a trademark of ASCD. The highly acclaimed framework is being piloted and implemented in schools and school districts across the nation.

Monroe received her EdD from Rowan University, her master's from Pratt Institute, and her bachelor's from the College of the Holy Cross.

Ruben Britt, Jr., is an educator, career coach, lecturer, and National Certified Counselor who has over forty-five years of experience in education as both a teacher and career planning counselor. A nationally recognized expert on issues related to education and career coaching, he has worked as a consultant for the U.S. Department of Education, the Educational Testing Service, the New Jersey Department of Higher Education, and several colleges and community organizations. He is the author of the books *Winter in America: The Social and Moral Decline of a Great Nation,*

Reflection and Restoration: Quotes for Self-Empowerment and Motivation, and *Black and Powerful: The Career Guide for Tomorrow's Top Leaders.* He is also the author of a children's book on cultural diversity entitled *Lakota.* Ruben wrote two chapters for the book *The Last Job Search Guide You'll Ever Need*: "Networking: A Proven Tool for Job Seekers," and "The Portfolio: Your Ticket to Successful Interviewing." He has written a number of articles related to education, career development, and social issues for such publications as *Black Issues*

in *Higher Education*, *Upscale Magazine*, *Black Enterprise*, the *Philadelphia Inquirer*, and *Diversity in Ed Magazine*. He received his associate degree from the College of the Sequoias, his bachelor's from Southern University, and his master's from Bloomsburg University. He is a native of Roxbury, Massachusetts, and he is presently a career planning coach at Rowan University and the host of Career Talk on WGLS-FM, a show offering tips and advice on career planning and finding employment.

Printed in the USA
CPSIA information can be obtained
at www.ICGtesting.com
LVHW010018051223
765498LV00019B/57